MW01127426

The Lindbergh Kidnapping

by Geoffrey A. Campbell

FAMOUS
TRIALS

LUCENT
BOOKS®

THOMSON
™
GALE

San Diego • Detroit • New York • San Francisco • Cleveland
New Haven, Conn. • Waterville, Maine • London • Munich

THOMSON

GALE

To my role models, Glenn, Mitzi, and Linda

On cover: A newspaper clipping from early March1932 spotlights the
desperate search for Charles A. Lindbergh Jr., son of the famous aviator.

LIBRARY OF CONGRESS CATALOGING-IN-PUBLICATION DATA

Campbell, Geoffrey A.
 The Lindbergh kidnapping / by Geoffrey A. Campbell.
  v. cm. —— (Famous trials)
Includes bibliographical references and index.
Summary: Describes the kidnapping of Charlie, the infant son of Charles and Anne
Lindbergh; the search for Charlie; the investigation into the child's death, leading
to the arrest of Bruno Richard Hauptmann; and Hauptmann's trial for murder.
Contents: Introduction: ". . .On the front page of a newspaper" — The crime of
the century — A trail of dead ends and false leads — An avalanche of evidence —
"Where are they getting these witnesses?" —"We find the defendant . . . guilty."
  ISBN 1-59018-267-7 (alk. paper)
 1. Lindbergh, Charles Augustus, 1930–1932—Kidnapping, 1932—Juvenile litera-
ture. 2. Lindbergh, Charles A. (Charles Augustus), 1902–1974—Juvenile literature.
3. Hauptmann, Bruno Richard, 1899–1936—Juvenile literature. 4. Kidnapping—New
Jersey—Juvenile literature. 5. Murder—New Jersey—Juvenile literature. 6. Trials
(Kidnapping)—New Jersey—Juvenile literature. 7. Trials (Murder)—New Jersey—
Juvenile literature. [1. Lindbergh, Charles Augustus, 1930–1932—Kidnapping),
1932. 2. Lindbergh, Charles A. (Charles Augustus), 1902–1974. 3. Hauptmann,
Bruno Richard, 1899–1936. 4. Kidnapping. 5. Murder. 6. Trials (Kidnapping) 7. Trials
(Murder)] I. Title. II. Series.
 HV6603.L5 C35 2003
 345.73'0254——dc21

                                                                    2002152982

Table of Contents

Foreword

"The law is not an end in and of itself, nor does it provide ends. It is preeminently a means to serve what we think is right."

William J. Brennan Jr.

THE CONCEPT OF JUSTICE AND THE RULE OF LAW are hallmarks of Western civilization, manifested perhaps most visibly in widely famous and dramatic court trials. These trials include such important and memorable personages as the ancient Greek philosopher Socrates, who was accused and convicted of corrupting the minds of his society's youth in 399 B.C.; the French maiden and military leader Joan of Arc, accused and convicted of heresy against the church in 1431; to former football star O.J. Simpson, acquitted of double murder in 1995. These and other well-known and controversial trials constitute the most public, and therefore most familiar, demonstrations of a Western legal tradition that dates back through the ages. Although no one is certain when the first law code appeared or when the first formal court trials were held, Babylonian ruler Hammurabi introduced the first known law code in about 1760 B.C. It remains unclear how this code was administered, and no records of specific trials have survived. What is clear, however, is that humans have always sought to govern behavior and define actions in terms of law.

Almost all societies have made laws and prosecuted people for going against those laws, but the question of which behaviors to sanction and which to censure has always been controversial and remains in flux. Some, such as Roman orator and legislator Cicero, argue that laws are simply applications of universal standards. Cicero believed that humanity would agree on what constituted illegal behavior and that human laws were a mere extension of natural laws. "True law is right reason in agreement with nature," he wrote,

world-wide in scope, unchanging, everlasting. . . . We
may not oppose or alter that law, we cannot abolish it, we
cannot be freed from its obligations by any legisla-
ture. . . . This [natural] law does not differ for Rome and
for Athens, for the present and for the future. . . . It is and
will be valid for all nations and all times.

Cicero's rather optimistic view has been contradicted
throughout history, however. For every law made to preserve har-
mony and set universal standards of behavior, another has been
born of fear, prejudice, greed, desire for power, and a host of
other motives. History is replete with individuals defying and
fighting to change such laws—and even to topple governments
that dictate such laws. Abolitionists fought against slavery, civil
rights leaders fought for equal rights, millions throughout the
world have fought for independence—these constitute a mini-
mum of reasons for which people have sought to overturn laws
that they believed to be wrong or unjust. In opposition to Cicero,
then, many others, such as eighteenth-century English poet and
philosopher William Godwin, believe humans must be con-
stantly vigilant against bad laws. As Godwin said in 1793:

Laws we sometimes call the wisdom of our ancestors.
But this is a strange imposition. It was as frequently the
dictate of their passion, of timidity, jealousy, a monopo-
lizing spirit, and a lust of power that knew no bounds.
Are we not obliged perpetually to renew and remodel
this misnamed wisdom of our ancestors? To correct it by
a detection of their ignorance, and a censure of their in-
tolerance?

Lucent Books' *Famous Trials* series showcases trials that exem-
plify both society's praiseworthy condemnation of universally un-
acceptable behavior and its misguided persecution of individuals
based on fear and ignorance, as well as trials that leave open the
question of whether justice has been done. Each volume begins by
setting the scene and providing a historical context to show how
society's mores influence the trial process and the verdict.

Each book goes on to present a detailed and lively account of the trial, including liberal use of primary source material such as direct testimony, lawyers' summations, and contemporary and modern commentary. In addition, sidebars throughout the text create a broader context by presenting illuminating details about important points of law, information on key personalities, and important distinctions related to civil, federal, and criminal procedures. Thus, all of the primary and secondary source material included in both the text and the sidebars demonstrates to readers the sources and methods historians use to derive information and conclusions about such events.

Lastly, each *Famous Trials* volume includes one or more of the following comprehensive tools that motivate readers to pursue further reading and research. A timeline allows readers to see the scope of the trial at a glance, annotated bibliographies provide both sources for further research and a thorough list of works consulted, a glossary helps students with unfamiliar words and concepts, and a comprehensive index permits quick scanning of the book as a whole.

The insight of Oliver Wendell Holmes Jr., distinguished Supreme Court justice, exemplifies the theme of the *Famous Trials* series. Taken from *The Common Law*, published in 1881, Holmes remarked: "The life of the law has not been logic, it has been experience." That "experience" consists mainly in how laws are applied in society and challenged in the courts, a process resulting in differing outcomes from one generation to the next. Thus, the *Famous Trials* series encourages readers to examine trials within a broader historical and social context.

Introduction

"On the Front Page of a Newspaper"

WHEN COLONEL CHARLES A. Lindbergh married Anne Spencer Morrow on May 27, 1929, all the world took note. Lindbergh had become a celebrity in 1927 when his specially built airplane, which he dubbed the *Spirit of St. Louis,* touched down in Paris. It was the first time anyone had flown alone across the Atlantic Ocean. For her part, Anne was a wealthy socialite, the daughter of investment banker and U.S. diplomat Dwight D. Morrow. The young couple was instantly the subject of relentless news coverage.

Reflecting on how they always had to be mindful of an aggressive press intent upon chronicling their every move together, Anne recalled that she felt "like a deer, hunted by smiling, smirking, sure-of-themselves, relentless hunters."[1] Lindbergh acknowledged the couple's life together would be difficult because of constant publicity. He once told Anne, "Never say anything you wouldn't want shouted from the housetops, and never write anything you wouldn't mind seeing on the front page of a newspaper."[2]

The Lindberghs lived for a time at the Morrow family's estate in Englewood, New Jersey, but the couple soon purchased a 390-acre tract of land straddling the Mercer County and Hunterdon County lines in the middle of New Jersey, a short distance from the town of Hopewell in a remote, heavily wooded area. By 1930, Charles and Anne Lindbergh had begun work on a fourteen-room home on the land. That same year, the couple celebrated the birth on June 22 of Charles Augustus Lindbergh Jr. While their hideaway was being built, they continued to live at the Morrow estate.

The remoteness of the property promised the Lindberghs seclusion and freedom from the press and curiosity seekers, since the only direct access to the Lindbergh home was over a dirt road. The respite from publicity was more than welcome to Anne Lindbergh, who in a letter to her mother wrote of her distress:

> I have gotten utterly bitter about it [the publicity]. I have no patience, no understanding, no sympathy with the people who stare and follow and giggle at us. . . . Oh, Mother, it is so wearing. I wonder if it will ever slacken. . . . It is like being born with no nose, or deformed— everyone on the streets looks at you once and then again; always looks back—that second look, the leer. No one

World-famous pilot Charles Lindbergh and his wife, Anne, pictured here soon after their marriage, endured intense media scrutiny.

else gets that. President Hoover doesn't get it; Daddy doesn't get it; they get a dignified curiosity. But that look, as though we were a public amusement, monkeys in a cage. There are so few people in the world who treat us naturally. . . . And then it works both ways; if they aren't natural, I can't be.[3]

By the spring of 1932, the Lindberghs were routinely spending weekends in their new home. On March 1, however, the Lindberghs' peace was ended by tragedy when their young son was kidnapped. Their hideaway was overrun with reporters, cameramen, and mere curiosity seekers, all of whom hoped to get a glimpse of the couple, whose storybook lives had been turned upside down. The ultimately fruitless attempts to retrieve Charles Lindbergh Jr. alive, along with the subsequent capture, trial, and execution of the person accused of the crime, would rivet the nation's attention for four long years.

Chapter 1

The Crime of the Century

ALTHOUGH BY THANKSGIVING 1931 their new home near the town of Hopewell, New Jersey, was basically finished, the Lindberghs still spent most of their time at the Morrow estate in Englewood, staying at what they called the farm only on weekends. The last weekend in February was different. On Monday, little Charlie, as he was known, was suffering from a cold that he

---

The Lindberghs' Hopewell home was built as a haven for the young family. Tragically, it became a crime scene when their baby, Charlie, was abducted.

had come down with over the weekend. Because it was a chilly, rainy day, the Lindberghs decided to keep the child where he was and stay at their new home at least through Tuesday. Charlie's Scottish-born nursemaid, twenty-eight-year-old Betty Gow, did not ordinarily accompany the Lindberghs to Hopewell. On their weekend trips to Hopewell, the Lindberghs were served by Oliver and Elsie Whateley, the butler and cook who lived at the Lindbergh property full-time. But Colonel Lindbergh, who was going to work in New York City for the day on Tuesday, made arrangements for Gow to drive on Tuesday morning from Engle-wood to the farm to help his wife, who was pregnant with the couple's second child, tend to Charlie.

On Tuesday afternoon, Gow played inside with Charlie while Anne took a walk. At 3:30, Anne found some pebbles and tossed them at the second-floor nursery windows. Gow came to the window holding Charlie, who smiled at the sight of his mother. Gow helped Charlie wave to Anne.

Charlie Is Prepared for Bed

By 6:00 P.M., Gow was feeding Charlie in the nursery. Anne came in to help prepare the baby for bed. Just before putting him in his crib, Gow gave Charlie some medicine for his cold, which he spit out on his nightclothes. Gow, an accomplished seamstress, removed his soiled clothing and decided to make Charlie a flannel shirt to wear for extra warmth. She quickly made a sleeveless shirt from a piece of flannel cloth, rubbed Charlie's chest with Vicks VapoRub, then put the new shirt on him. She put a store-bought shirt over her creation. Charlie was already wearing a rubber-covered diaper. The baby was dressed in one more piece of outerwear, a one-piece sleeper, then placed in bed and covered with a blanket.

Anne closed the window shutters. The shutters on the south wall, along with the shutters on the north side of the nursery's east wall, were tightly closed. However, the shutters on the south-east window were warped. Anne could not bring them together tightly enough to lock them. She switched off the nursery light and went to the first floor, while Gow remained in the nursery. At

THE LINDBERGH KIDNAPPING

Betty Gow, the Lindberghs' nursemaid, made the devastating discovery that little Charlie had vanished.

8:00 P.M., she went downstairs and told Anne that Charlie was resting peacefully and then withdrew to have dinner with Elsie Whately. Oliver Whately was in the pantry.

A half-hour later, Charles Lindbergh returned home. After greeting the servants, he joined Anne for dinner. Around 9:00 P.M., the couple finished eating and retired to the living room. Lindbergh was startled by a noise he thought sounded like slats from an orange crate falling to the kitchen floor. But the Lindberghs let the sound pass and chatted about the day. Charles then took a bath before going to his den, which was located directly underneath Charlie's room. Anne then bathed.

"They've Stolen Our Baby!"

At 10:00 P.M., Gow went to check on Charlie. After plugging in a small electric heater to warm the room, she went to the crib. She did not hear the baby breathe and became alarmed. As Gow later recalled, "I thought that something had happened to him, that perhaps the clothes had got over his head. In the half-light I saw he wasn't there, and felt all over the bed for him."[4] Gow ran to find Mrs. Lindbergh, but Anne did not have the baby. Gow then searched out Colonel Lindbergh to see if he had the child.

The two raced to the nursery. Lindbergh inspected the crib, then blurted, "Anne! They've stolen our baby!"[5] Anne Lindbergh's startled response was a simple, "Oh, my God!"[6] Colonel Lindbergh noticed that the right-hand shutter of the southeast window was open and that the window was raised. On top of a radiator case by the window, he saw a white envelope, but, assuming that the envelope contained a ransom demand, Lindbergh left the envelope untouched so as not to mar any fingerprints. Anne Lindbergh frantically searched the room.

THE LITTLE EAGLE

Charles A. Lindbergh Jr. was a darling of the public from birth, and interest in the son of the famous aviator was intense. Photos of the child and newsreels featuring Charlie were shown in movie theaters around the nation.

News of the baby's kidnapping understandably aroused the sympathy of the nation. On March 3, the *New York Times* chronicled the public outpouring of sorrow. As related on the *Times'* website at www.nytimes.com:

> The entire nation extended its sympathy to Colonel and Mrs. Charles A. Lindbergh yesterday. From President Hoover down, all were awaiting anxiously the latest news of the kidnapped child. They talked about it in the streets, in homes and in their offices. Many formal prayers were offered, and many more informal ones voiced the hope that the boy would be returned safely to his home. In Europe, also, where lengthy accounts of the kidnapping were published, widespread sympathy was expressed.

As the Lindberghs had already learned, however, their celebrity was a double-edged sword. While capable of arousing the deepest sympathy from both leaders and ordinary citizens from around the world,

the Lindberghs were the subject of constant media scrutiny. As a particularly egregious example of the lengths to which people went to chronicle the family, photographers sneaked into the morgue where Charlie's body lay and photographed his corpse.

Young Charlie on his first birthday. Within months, he would disappear.

Colonel Lindbergh grabbed a rifle, instructed everyone not to touch the white envelope, and headed out into the dark night. He walked only about one hundred feet along the dirt road in front of the house before deciding that since he had no flashlight, his search would be futile. He returned to the house and phoned the authorities; he also called his friend and lawyer, Henry Breckinridge.

"The Child Is in Gut Care"

When the police and Breckinridge arrived, Lindbergh made it clear that his priority was the safe return of Charlie. He wanted the police to process the crime scene and to pursue any leads. However, he did not want the police to hinder his efforts to get in touch with the kidnappers and secure the return of his son. The Lindberghs went so far as to tell the police they did not care if the kidnapper or kidnappers were caught, so long as they were able to get Charlie back. With that understanding, the ransom envelope was dusted for fingerprints. Only a smudge appeared. Inside was a single sheet of paper. Handwritten in blue ink, the message read in illiterate English,

> Dear Sir!
> Have 50,000$ redy 25000$ in 20$ bills 15000$ in 10$ bills and 10000$ in 5$ bils.
> After 2–4 days we wil inform you were to deliver theMony.
> We warn you for making anyding public or for the polise the child is in gut care.
> Indication for all letters are signature and 3 holes.[7]

The "signature" meant by the writer was apparently an odd symbol, appearing at the bottom of the note, which consisted of two interlocking circles. In the oval formed where the circles overlapped was a solid red mark. Three small holes had been punched through the symbol. Police dusted the note itself for prints but did not even find a smudge. The police did, however, make an important discovery when searching the grounds of the Lindbergh property. Below the nursery window, the officers found indentations in the mud that appeared to have been made

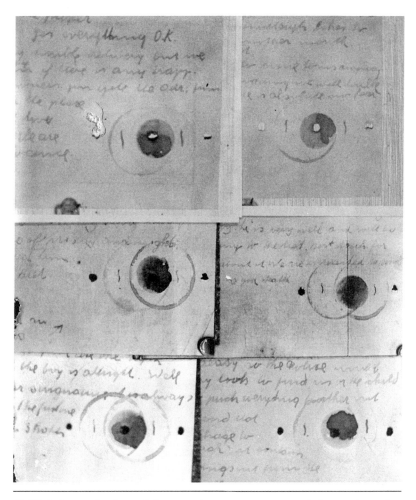

Published reproductions of the mysterious ransom note symbols are pictured here. The "signatures" containing two interlocking circles are clearly visible.

by a ladder. Following a set of footprints, the officers discovered a homemade ladder in two sections about seventy-five feet from the house. Another ten feet away they found a third section to the ladder. There was no sign of Charlie Lindbergh.

Breaking the News

Within hours the kidnapping became national news. As police combed the Lindbergh property, the story dominated radio and newspapers across the country. On March 3, NBC radio broad-cast a message on behalf of the Lindberghs, in which the couple stated that they wanted to get in touch with the kidnappers as soon as possible. The Lindberghs promised to keep their negoti-ations secret from the police. They said they were not interested in seeing anyone punished for the crime and that their only in-terest was Charlie's safe return. Meanwhile, Anne Lindbergh worried that the kidnappers would not properly care for Charlie. She wrote out Charlie's diet, which promptly appeared on the front pages of newspapers across the nation.

On Friday, March 4, the Lindberghs wrote an open letter that also appeared nationally. It read,

> Mrs. Lindbergh and I desire to make personal contact with the kidnappers of our child. Our only interest is in his immediate and safe return. We feel certain that the kidnappers will realize that this interest is strong enough to justify them in having complete confidence and trust in any promise that we may make in connection with his return. We urge those who have the child to send any representatives that they may desire to meet a represen-tative of ours who will be suitable to them at any time and at any place they may designate.

> If this is accepted we promise that we will keep what-ever arrangements may be made by their representatives and ours strictly confidential and we further pledge our-selves that we will not try to injure in any way those con-nected with the return of the child.[8]

A Second Note

That day, the Lindberghs received a second note from the kid-nappers. It included the odd symbol that had appeared on the first note, convincing Lindbergh that the letter was genuine. The note expressed disapproval of the Lindberghs for having notified the police and said that the resulting intense police ac-tivity meant that a meeting would not be possible until "every-thing is quite."[9] The letter assured the couple that Charlie would be cared for and fed "according to the diet," [10] thrilling Anne because it meant that the kidnappers had seen her plea in the papers. The note also said that because of the police activity and the kidnappers' need to keep Charlie longer than expected, the ransom was being increased to $70,000.

At this point, a seventy-two-year-old part-time lecturer at Fordham University named John F. Condon entered the scene. Although Condon did not know the Lindberghs personally, he idolized Colonel Lindbergh because of his famous trans-Atlantic flight and had avidly followed the publicity surrounding the case. Condon wanted to do something to help. On his own initiative he placed a letter in the March 8 edition of the *Bronx Home News,* offering to serve as an intermediary between the kidnappers and the Lindberghs. His letter said in part,

> I offer all I can scrape together so a loving mother may again have her child and Colonel Lindbergh may know that the American people are grateful for the honor bestowed upon them by his pluck and daring.

> Let the kidnapers know that no testimony of mine, or information coming from me, will be used against them. I offer $1000.00, which I've saved from my salary (all my life's savings), in addition to the suggested $50,000. I am ready, at my own expense, to go anywhere, also to give the kidnapers the extra money and never utter their names to anyone. [11]

The next day, Condon received a letter in the mail. The handwritten letter said,

> dear Sir: if you are willing to act as go-between in the Lindbergh case please follow strictly instruction. Handel incloced letter personaly to Mr. Lindbergh. It will explain everything. don't tell anyone about it as soon we find out the press or Police is notified everything are cancell and it will be a further delay. After you get the money from Mr. Lindbergh put these 3 words in the New-York American[.]

BOGUS LEADS AND OFFERS OF HELP

Even as the Lindberghs pursued negotiations with what they believed to be the kidnappers via John Condon, they also examined several other claims from people either claiming to have seen Charlie with the kidnappers or from those who said they could help negotiate the return of the baby to the Lindberghs. One offer of help came from the notorious Al Capone, a Chicago gangster who was in jail serving an eleven-year sentence for income tax evasion.

As related in George Waller's *Kidnap: The Story of the Lindbergh Case,* Capone offered a $10,000 reward for the baby's safe return, saying, "It's the most outrageous thing I ever heard of. I know how Mrs. Capone and I would feel if our son were [kidnapped], and I sympathize with the Lindberghs. If I were out of jail I could be of real assistance. I have friends all over the country who could aid in running this thing down." Although Lindbergh, grasping at any possible means of hope for his child, was reportedly intrigued by the offer, he never seriously considered asking authorities to free Capone to aid in the search.

However, Lindbergh did authorize negotiations between Evalyn McLean, a wealthy socialite, and Gaston Means, an ex-FBI agent who subsequently became a con man. Means bilked McLean out of more than $100,000. He told McLean that he was in contact with the kidnappers, who had demanded the $100,000 ransom for the Lindbergh baby's safe return. Lindbergh also treated seriously claims by John Hughes Curtis, a Norfolk shipbuilder, that he was in contact with the kidnappers. Curtis claimed the kidnappers were keeping Charlie on a boat off the Atlantic coast, near Cape May, New Jersey.

Mony is redy After notise we will give you further instruction. don't be affraid we are not out for your 1000$ keep it. Only act stricly. Be at home every night between 6–12 by this time you will hear from us. [12]

A smaller envelope was enclosed, with a note directing Condon to hand deliver the enclosure to Lindbergh and with an admonition that it "is in Mr. Lindbergh interest not to notify the Police." [13]

"Money Is Ready"

Condon contacted Lindbergh, who invited the retired schoolteacher to the Hopewell home. After reviewing the enclosure, which included the distinctive symbol of interlocking circles and punched holes, Lindbergh was convinced of the letter's authenticity. The letter stated that Condon was acceptable as a go-between and that once the money was received, the Lindberghs would be given instructions on where to find their baby. Condon spent the night at the Lindberghs', sleeping on the nursery floor. The next day, Lindbergh, Breckinridge, and Condon readied the ad to run in the *New York American* as stipulated by the kidnapper. But they did not know how to sign the letter. They worried that if the message contained Condon's name, he would become besieged by reporters and the kidnappers would be scared off, causing further delay. Putting Condon's initials—JFC—together, they came up with the code name of Jafsie. On Friday, March 11, the *New York American* contained Dr. Condon's ad: "MONEY IS READY. Jafsie."[14]

The next evening, Condon received a letter instructing him to bring the money with him to a spot near a New York subway line stop. Condon did not have the money, and Breckinridge, who was at Condon's home at the time, worried that the kidnappers would be angered. But Condon believed he could explain the circumstances to the kidnappers. In the meantime, he believed, it was important to follow the letter's instructions. Once he arrived, he found another note at an abandoned hot dog stand instructing him to cross the street and walk next to the fence enclosing Woodlawn Cemetery. After waiting more than fifteen minutes, Condon was greeted by a shadowy man on the other side of the fence. The man asked Condon if he had the money. Condon replied that he could not bring the money until he saw the baby.

At that moment a cemetery guard happened by, so the two left together, continuing their conversation at Van Cortlandt Park. At Condon's insistence, the man, who identified himself as "John," assured him that Charlie was safe. Then Condon asked the man for details about the plot. He was told that Charlie was on a boat about six hours away and that the kidnapping gang consisted of six people, including two nurses for the baby. John promised to send a token to reassure the Lindberghs of Charlie's well-being, saying that Condon could expect to soon receive the baby's sleeper.

"The Baby Is Well"

On Monday, an ad written by Condon and Breckinridge appeared in the *Bronx Home News*. It read, "Money is ready. No cops. No Secret Service. No press. I come alone, like last time. Jafsie." [15] On Tuesday, Condon received a soft package wrapped in brown paper. He took it unopened to Breckinridge's office, where the parcel was opened. Inside was a folded baby garment, a one-piece sleeping suit with closed feet. Attached was a note with writing on both sides. The note said the kidnappers would not allow anyone to see the baby until after the ransom had been received. Apparently sensing that Lindbergh was uncertain whether he was

JAFSIE

One of the most intriguing characters in the Lindbergh case was Dr. John F. Condon, whose desire to help the Lindberghs led him to place an ad in an obscure newspaper. The note eventually brought him into contact with the Lindbergh baby kidnapper. Self-assured and certain of his own importance, Condon added a wrinkle to a case already well peopled with characters.

In *The Airman and the Carpenter: The Lindbergh Kidnapping and the Framing of Richard Hauptmann*. Ludovic Kennedy describes the seventy two-year-old Condon:

> He was 6 foot 2, weighed 200 pounds and was a physical fitness buff. He had a white mane of hair, a large white walrus moustache, and wore a black derby or bowler hat, like any English city gent. He thought and never tired of saying that America was the finest country in the world and the Bronx the most beautiful borough in it. "Every Fourth of July," wrote one observer, "he hit the outdoor festival circuit and, sweating in a dark winter suit, sang "The Star-Spangled Banner." Many adjectives have been used to describe Dr Condon: chauvinistic, sentimental, garrulous, sycophantic, histrionic, patronizing, pseudo-humble; above all anxious to see himself and be seen by others in the best possible light.

John F. Condon.

dealing with the true kidnappers, the note pointed out the unique signature, which "is always the same as the first one" [16]—the interlocking circles and three punched holes.

On the other side of the paper, the note continued with hopeful news. The kidnappers urged that Mrs. Lindbergh be reassured that "the baby is well." [17] However, the letter concluded with a request that Lindbergh place an ad in the newspaper advising whether he was willing to pay the full $70,000 in ransom.

Lindbergh soon arrived and identified the sleeper as Charlie's. The three men hammered out a response to the note. On March 17, both the *Bronx Home News* and *New York American* contained the following message: "I accept. Money is ready. John, your package is delivered and is O.K. Direct me. Jafsie." [18]

Plans Finalized

On April 1, after what seemed to Condon and Lindbergh an interminable delay, Condon received a note from the kidnapper. It had an enclosure that Condon was instructed to deliver to Lindbergh. The enclosure directed Lindbergh to have the money ready by the next day, a Saturday. Future communications would tell him where the money should be taken. The note promised that eight hours after the money was received, Lindbergh would be notified where he could find the baby.

In the meantime, Elmer Irey of the Internal Revenue Service contacted Lindbergh. He noted that because of an impending change in the government's monetary policy, gold coins and currency known as gold certificates would be recalled. Irey believed that including gold certificates in the ransom payment, and recording the serial numbers of all the bills in the ransom package, would greatly enhance the ability of law enforcement agents to track down the kidnappers. Lindbergh, after some reluctance, agreed. Irey assembled $70,000 in ransom money, which included a large proportion of gold certificates that would be relatively easy to spot, especially as gold certificates became less common. All the serial numbers on the ransom bills were recorded. A pamphlet listing all the serial numbers in the ransom package was printed and distributed to banks and businesses.

On April 2, Lindbergh and Breckinridge patiently waited with the ransom money at Condon's house. At 7:45 P.M., the doorbell rang. A cabdriver had left an envelope. Condon tore it open. Inside were instructions to a nearby florist shop, where further instructions were hidden. The note directed Condon to bring the ransom money with him and warned against bringing the police.

"Hey, Doctor!"

Lindbergh and Condon set out immediately. At the florist shop Condon found the promised note of instructions. It directed him

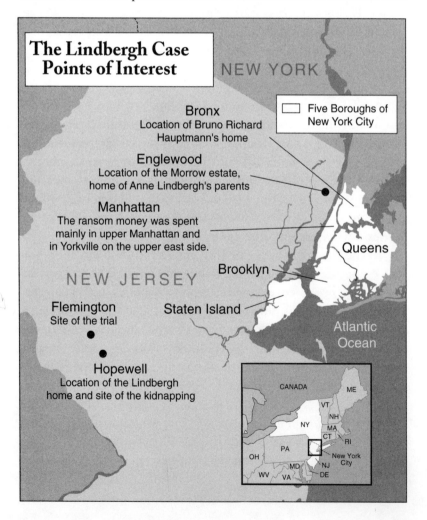

**The Lindbergh Case
Points of Interest**

NEW YORK

Bronx
Location of Bruno Richard
Hauptmann's home

☐ Five Boroughs of
New York City

Englewood
Location of the Morrow estate,
home of Anne Lindbergh's parents

Manhattan
The ransom money was spent
mainly in upper Manhattan and
in Yorkville on the upper east side.

Queens

NEW JERSEY

Brooklyn

Flemington
Site of the trial

Staten Island

Atlantic
Ocean

Hopewell
Location of the Lindbergh
home and site of the kidnapping

CANADA

ME

VT

NH

NY

MA

CT

RI

OH

PA

New York
City

WV

MD

NJ

VA

DE

to cross the street, the site of St. Raymond's Cemetery, where the kidnapper would meet him. Condon told Lindbergh he would come back for the money later and set out for his meeting. After waiting without contact, he became alarmed and began to think no one was coming. Just as he was about to give up, a voice called from the darkness. "Hey, Doctor!"[19] Both Lindbergh and Condon heard the voice, and Condon recognized the voice as that of John. Condon followed the voice and, behind some shrubs, came upon a man wearing a hat and a black suit. The men talked briefly, and Condon demanded instructions for finding the baby. John agreed to provide these once Condon gave him the money. Condon went to the car to get the cash, while John went away to write a receipt and the directions to Charlie's location.

The exchange was made. John took the money and disappeared into St. Raymond's Cemetery. Condon went back to the car with the note. The note said Charlie was on a small, twenty-eight-foot boat, spelled "Boad,"[20] named the *Nelly*, which was off the coast of Massachusetts near Elizabeth Island.

Lindbergh lined up an amphibious aircraft to use for the search for the *Nelly*. The search, however, proved fruitless. Lindbergh saw no boat that matched the description of the *Nelly* and realized he had been tricked. Nevertheless, the Lindberghs tried to reestablish contact with the kidnappers via ads in the local papers.

William Allen's Discovery

The Lindberghs' last hope that they might see Charlie alive was dashed around 3:15 P.M. on May 12, when a truck driver named William Allen pulled over to the side of the road. He had to relieve himself and decided to walk into the woods to tend to his needs. The spot he chose happened to be no more than two miles from the Lindbergh home. While ducking to avoid a low branch, he noticed a baby's head in the dirt below. He quickly notified authorities. Although the body was in an advanced state of decay, police noticed the blond hair and saw a dimple on the chin. Police instantly believed they had found Charlie but delayed making a formal announcement. They asked Gow for a remnant of the cloth from the shirt she had made Charlie on the night of the kidnapping, and that sample matched a shirt still on the corpse. Colonel Lindbergh and Gow later made a positive identification of the body. Fearing that a grave would be ransacked by souvenir hunters and otherwise desecrated, the grieving Lindberghs made arrangements to have their son cremated.

Chapter 2

A Trail
of Dead Ends
and False Leads

WITHIN HOURS OF the first police call on March 1, the Lindbergh kidnapping had become national news. Hordes of reporters, photographers, curiosity seekers, and souvenir hunters descended upon the Lindbergh estate. The throng initially impeded the police investigation, which was under way even as Lindbergh attempted to negotiate with the kidnappers. However, the police eventually regained control of the crime scene, though no one can say how much evidence was lost or destroyed in the initial mayhem.

The public's appetite for news about the case was insatiable. Typical of the early coverage of the kidnapping, on March 2 the *New York Times* reported,

> Charles Augustus Lindbergh Jr., 20-month-old son of Colonel and Mrs. Charles A. Lindbergh, was kidnapped between 8:30 and 10 o'clock last night from his crib in the nursery on the second floor of his parents' home at Hopewell, near Princeton, N.J.
>
> ... "I hope you boys will excuse me," Colonel Lindbergh explained to the reporters, "but I would rather the State Police answered all questions. I am sure you understand how I feel." Mrs. Lindbergh, though greatly shocked by

25

the baby's disappearance, was reported to be bearing up as well as could be expected.[21]

One of the first things police did was to establish a vast drag-net across the region as law enforcement agencies sought to quickly apprehend the kidnappers and return the baby to the Lindberghs. The police already had one lead: A workman along a highway that ran near the Lindbergh estate told them that a dark-colored sedan with New York plates had stopped, and the two men inside had asked for directions to the Lindberghs' home. Still, police stopped many cars, regardless of the description. Drifters, people with criminal records, and anyone deemed the slightest bit suspicious were questioned by police throughout the area.

Not long after the first report of the kidnapping reached police, representatives of the New Jersey State Police arrived. The first was Corporal Joseph A. Wolf, who got to the Lindbergh estate at 10:55 P.M. Wolf received a quick briefing on the evening's events from Lindbergh and then relayed them to headquarters. Wolf then went to the nursery and, using a penknife, moved the

---

The kidnapper entered Charlie's nursery through this window and departed the same way, with the child in his arms.

ransom note to a fireplace mantle. The men then returned downstairs, where Wolf questioned Lindbergh in more depth before going outside to examine the ground underneath the nursery window. He found a chisel in the mud and then examined the footprint. Although no one had a tape measure, the print was estimated at twelve and one-half inches long and about four and one-quarter inches wide. Meanwhile, more state police officers continued to arrive, one of whom discovered a set of tire tracks on a dirt road near the Lindbergh home.

Crime Scene Processed

Around midnight, Colonel H. Norman Schwarzkopf, the head of the New Jersey Police, and his number two man, Major Charles Schoeffel, arrived. Corporal Frank Kelly of the state police was taken to the nursery to dust for fingerprints. He dusted the crib, walls, and window glass. He took photos of the room and took samples of dirt found on the floor underneath the window. He eventually turned his attention to the ladder and to the chisel that had been found underneath the nursery window. Kelly was unable to turn up any identifiable prints. Kelly's initial investigative report outlined the police's early understanding of the crime. Police speculated that a group of two or more people drove close to the Lindbergh home, parked out of sight, and approached the home carrying a three-piece homemade extension ladder. Police believed one of the kidnappers had leaned the ladder against the Lindbergh home, used it to climb up to Charlie's second-story room, entered a window, kidnapped the child, and left as he had entered.

Police were active not just in Hopewell; officers across the nation responded to tips from well-intentioned citizens about suspicious people seen with twenty-month-old babies. Everywhere, the police were vigilant. One hapless Trenton, New Jersey, banker, making a cross-country vacation by car, was stopped and questioned by police 107 times because his vehicle bore New Jersey license plates.

In just the first few weeks of the police investigation into the kidnapping, the New Jersey State Police received and checked out more than two hundred thousand leads. Meanwhile, the Federal Bureau of Investigation had checked fifty thousand and the New York City Police another sixteen thousand. The leads were invariably dead ends, or outright lies. Shortly after the kidnapping, for example, the Lindberghs received a postcard that read, "Baby safe. Wait instructions later. Act accordingly." [22] After tracking down the store from which the postcard had been purchased and getting a description of the purchaser, the Newark police found not the kidnapper but a mentally ill boy.

Leading Suspects

At the outset, the police acted on the assumption that anyone was capable of the crime. Not surprisingly, their initial focus was on the servants and employees of the Lindbergh and Morrow families—people who would have knowledge of the Lindberghs' routines and whereabouts.

The first suspect considered was Betty Gow, the nursemaid. She was, after all, the last to have seen the baby and was also one of the few people who knew that the Lindberghs would even be in their new home on Tuesday. On March 3, Lieutenant Arthur T. Keaten of the state police detective bureau, questioned Gow about the evening's events. However, nothing she said aroused real suspicion, and investigators

Nursemaid Betty Gow, the last person to see Charlie, became the first suspect in the kidnapping.

Suspect Violet Sharpe, the Morrows' maid, was openly hostile to police.

were convinced of her very real concern for the welfare of the child.

The police also interviewed servants working at the Morrow family estate in Englewood, since they too would have known of the Lindberghs' plans. Violet Sharpe, the Morrow's maid, was of particular interest. Not only did Sharpe indicate that she resented being questioned, but police found her evasive and hostile. Finally, Sharpe admitted that on February 28, as she walked down an Englewood street with her sister, she had waved at a man in a passing car. The man stopped and offered the women a ride home. That evening, Sharpe went on a movie date with the man and another couple, returning home at 11:00 P.M. Sharpe, however, claimed not to remember the man's name or the movie they had seen. When pressed for details, she exclaimed, "You have no business prying into my private life!"[23]

Sharpe Raises Suspicion

Sharpe was reinterviewed on April 13. She was more cooperative this time and said that her earlier statement that she had gone to a movie was incorrect. In fact, she, her date, and the other couple had gone to a bar called the Peanut Grill. Sharpe also recalled that the man's first name was Ernie, though she said she could not remember his last name. The police were frustrated. Sharpe's answers only raised more questions. For example, Sharpe had been dating Septimus Banks, the Morrow family butler, and there were rumors among the other Morrow servants that the couple were to be married. Why, then, the police wondered, would Sharpe go on a date with a man who picked her up off the street? Moreover, Sharpe's sister, Emily, had returned to England. She had applied for a visa to return to England on the day of the kidnapping, and on April 6, just four days after the ransom payment, had gone back home.

Sharpe was interviewed a third time on June 9. Confronted with a photo of a petty thief named Ernest Brinkert, Sharpe said that the photo was of the "Ernie" with whom she had gone to the bar on the evening of the kidnapping. The detective questioning Sharpe asked a number of follow-up questions, but Sharpe began sobbing uncontrollably. A doctor was summoned, who urged that questioning be brought to a halt. The detective said questioning would resume the following day. Shockingly, however, the next day Sharpe committed suicide by drinking a cyanide potion. Moreover, the police located Brinkert, who vehemently denied knowing Sharpe. To further complicate matters, a man named Ernest Miller voluntarily came forward to announce that he was the man who had gone out with Sharpe on the night of the kidnapping. His story checked out. Authorities never were able to determine why Sharpe gave such wildly contradictory accounts of her activities or whether she was, in some way, connected to the kidnapping. Nevertheless, the trail investigators' hope to travel via Sharpe to the Lindbergh kidnappers had proved to be nothing more than a cul-de-sac, and the investigation floundered.

Investigators next turned their attention to Condon, whom they aggressively grilled on June 16. However, Condon never backed away from his assertion that he had acted as an intermediary only as a token of his respect for Lindbergh and his desire to see Charlie back in his mother's arms. Police later made an extensive search of Condon's home and yard but found nothing to link him to the crime.

Wood Expert Consulted

Out of new leads and no closer to discovering the identity of the kidnappers, Schwarzkopf sent a trooper to England to do a thorough background check of the Morrow servants. Working with detectives at the New Scotland Yard, the trooper was unable to find any connection between the servants and the kidnapping.

Investigators started taking a hard look at key physical evidence. One priority was the crude ladder found near the Lindberghs' house. Schwarzkopf sought out the services of Arthur Koehler, head of the U.S. Department of Agriculture's Forest Service Laboratory in Madison, Wisconsin. Koehler was an acknowledged expert on wood identification and wood construction, and Schwarzkopf thought Koehler might be able to unravel the origin of the wood used to make the ladder. Schwarzkopf believed that

AN ENRAGED PUBLIC

When the body of Charles A. Lindbergh Jr. was discovered a short distance from the Lindberghs' home, the nature of the police investigation changed substantially. The police were no longer looking for kidnappers and a baby. They were looking for murderers. The public, which had shown an outpouring of sympathy for the Lindberghs earlier, now wanted revenge.

According to *Kidnap: The Story of the Lindbergh Case* by George Waller, the *New York Daily News* captured the nation's mood perfectly when it wrote,

The kidnaped Lindbergh baby has been found—slain.

The damnable fiends, the inhuman monsters, who kidnaped the baby and presumably were responsible for the bilking of Colonel Lindbergh out of $50,000 are still at large.

Until the killers are tracked down and brought to justice, the children of America will not be safe. And the rest of the world will be able to point to this country and say: "That is the country where criminals can persecute decent citizens in absolute defiance of the law."

Does the Federal Government wish to preserve its integrity and its dignity, and so preserve the power of all other governmental agencies in this country?

If it does, it will put its best men on the trail of these fiends, and keep them on the trail until the fiends are captured and convicted of first degree murder.

The American people, shocked and grieved, will, we believe, demand such action by the Government in a voice that cannot be ignored.

if Koehler could track down where the wood came from, authorities would be able to narrow their search for the kidnapper.

Koehler studied the ladder with great precision. He even went so far as to label each of the ladder's parts for easy reference and identification. The ladder's rungs were numbered from one to eleven, and the side trails of the three sections were numbered twelve through seventeen. By March 4, 1933, he was ready to write a report. He noted such details as that rails twelve, thirteen, and sixteen had been made of North Carolina yellow pine, while rails fourteen, fifteen, and seventeen were made of Douglas fir. Of the ladder's construction, Koehler wrote, "The construction in general is very crude, showing poor judgment in the selection of the lumber and in the design of the ladder, and poor workmanship . . . very little skill or care in the use of carpenter tools." [24] Moreover, Koehler judged by the wide spacing between the rungs that the ladder was not intended for general use. In addition, there was no wear on the rungs, demonstrating that the ladder had not been used very often.

Rail Sixteen

One of Koehler's most intriguing findings was that rail sixteen, a side rail in the top section of the ladder, had previously been a board used for another purpose. He hypothesized that rail sixteen had been "in the interior of a crude building, possibly an attic, shop, warehouse, or barn." [25] Koehler noted that rail sixteen had four slanting nail holes, which had been made by square nails. However, he was unable to determine by the spacing of the holes what the board might have been used for, prior to serving as the ladder's side rail.

After examining the ladder's wood under a microscope, Koehler also discovered that rails twelve and thirteen had telltale marks made by the milling machine that processed the boards. Because the marks were so distinctive, Koehler believed that only one lumber mill could have produced the boards. That mill, he thought, would have records of where the wood had been shipped. Consequently, he might with some precision be able to determine the area in which the ladder was assembled.

Arthur Koehler inspects the ladder used by the kidnapper. He determined that the ladder was made of wood purchased from a Bronx lumberyard.

Although it was something of a long shot, Koehler wrote to lumber mills across the country, asking if any of their machines had defective knives that could have made the marks in question. Eventually he found that the boards in question had been milled by the M.G. and J.J. Dorn Lumber Company in McCormick, South Carolina. Moreover, the lumber had been sent to thirty lumberyards on the East Coast of the United States. After visiting all thirty lumberyards, Koehler finally found what he had been looking for. At the National Lumber and Millwork Company in the Bronx, he found several lengths of board containing the same distinctive marks as those on rails twelve and thirteen. Although Koehler had accomplished a relatively amazing feat, the discovery merely suggested that the person who built the ladder used in the kidnapping may have purchased the wood at the Bronx lumberyard. Further investigative work was needed before investigators could close in on the kidnapper.

Ransom Money Breaks Case Open

In the meantime, handwriting analysts were hard at working poring over the ransom letters. Schwarzkopf first sent the ransom notes to Wilmer T. Souder, who headed the National Bureau of Standards in Washington, D.C. Souder was a handwriting expert, and after examining the notes, he concluded that they were all the work of one person. Schwarzkopf then sent the letters to Albert Sherman Osborn, a private handwriting expert in New York City. Osborn agreed that one person had written all of the ransom notes. Among other things, some words were consistently misspelled. For example, the word "boat" was spelled "boad," and "signature" was spelled "singnature." Osborn also thought the grammar of the notes indicated that the writer was a native speaker of German.

The real break in the case came as a result of the ransom money. On April 5, 1933, President Franklin D. Roosevelt had ordered that all Americans who had gold bullion, gold coins, or gold certificates valued in excess of one hundred dollars to de-

HANDWRITING EVIDENCE

During the course of negotiations with Colonel Lindbergh, the kidnapper had written a total of fifteen ransom notes. At points during the investigation, these notes were among the only clues the police had.

The notes were turned over to psychiatrists as well as handwriting experts, more formally known as questioned documents examiners. These experts developed a fairly detailed picture of the person they believed had written the letters. Albert S. Osborn, the preeminent authority on questioned documents in the United States, studied the notes and concluded they were all written by the same person. Dr. Dudley D. Shoenfeld, a psychiatrist, concluded after reading the notes that the author was probably a German in his forties with a criminal past. As detailed in the *Hunterdon County Democrat*, found at Hunterdon Online, www.lindberghtrial.com, Shoenfeld "went on to add that the culprit was secretive to the point of paranoia, probably committed the crime alone, was mechanically skilled and unlikely to confess."

Taken individually, none of the handwriting analyses proved anything. However, authorities were nonetheless confident they had the right man when they arrested Bruno Richard Hauptmann. Coupled with other evidence in the case, the clues gleaned from the handwriting analyses appeared to authorities to clearly implicate Hauptmann in the crime.

posit them at a Federal Reserve bank prior to May 1, 1933. The executive order was designed to prevent Americans from hoarding gold, which many had done as the nation's economic collapse, known as the Great Depression, worsened. Because much of the Lindbergh ransom money had been in the form of gold certificates —currency that was redeemable for a like amount of gold—and because such bills were relatively rare and would become much more so with Roosevelt's order, authorities believed they might be able to capture the kidnappers when they tried to spend the ransom money. Indeed, bills from the ransom money had been turning up, and Detective James Finn of the New York City Police and Special Agent Thomas Sisk of the FBI had been keeping a map of all the places this had occurred. During the first few months, however, they were not able to find anyone who remembered how the money came into their possession.

As Finn and Sisk suspected, Roosevelt's order created a flurry of activity, and more bills from the ransom began showing up. In late April 1933, clerks at Chemical National Bank found fifty of the $10 ransom bills, and a few days later another fifty ransom bills in both $5 and $10 denominations showed up at Manufacturers Trust Company. However, nobody could remember the identity of the person who had exchanged the gold certificates for the newer currency. On May 1, a man went to the Federal Reserve bank in New York and turned in $2,980 in gold notes, each of which was part of the Lindbergh ransom note package. The only hint of the man's identity was a deposit slip. But when authorities went to the address listed on the deposit slip, they found the information had been a fabrication.

Store Clerks Provide a Physical Description

The bills were also being spent in stores, and as time passed it became clear the money was being spent almost exclusively in two areas of New York—in a strip of upper Manhattan and in a neighborhood of German immigrants known as Yorkville. Whenever a ransom bill turned up, Finn would try to get a description from store clerks of the person who had spent it. Although he often was unsuccessful, a number of cashiers clearly recalled the spender. They consistently described a white, blue-eyed man with high cheekbones who spoke with a German accent and wore a hat pulled down over his forehead. The description matched that given by Condon of his "Cemetery John." Another clue was that every bill had been folded in a peculiar way so that it had creases dividing it into eight sections.

By a March 1934, ransom bills were still turning up with regularity —at a rate of about forty dollars a week. The New York Police offered a five-dollar reward for every person who turned in a ransom bill, and Finn sent out a letter to gas stations in the city asking that attendants write down the license number of anyone using a gold note to pay for their gas. The letter said attendants could simply write the car's license number on the bills themselves.

On September 18, 1934, an alert teller at the Corn Exchange Bank in New York discovered a ten-dollar gold certificate among the day's deposits. Checking the serial number against the ransom bill circular, the teller found that it was one of the Lindbergh bills. The teller called the FBI, which notified officers from the New York City and New Jersey State Police departments. When the law enforcement authorities met at the bank, they found a notation on the margin of the bill. It read "4U-13-14 N.Y." Recalling Sisk's letter to gasoline stations, the officers believed this notation represented a license plate number. The officers canvassed several gas stations and came upon the Warren-Quinlan gas station in upper Manhattan. The manager and assistant both remembered the man who had paid with the gold certificate. The driver was white, spoke with a German accent, and drove a blue Dodge. Meanwhile, Finn checked out the license plate number with the motor vehicle bureau and discovered that the car was registered to Bruno Richard Hauptmann, a Bronx resident of German birth. The registration also included the information that Hauptmann was a carpenter and that his car was a dark blue Dodge.

Officials could find no criminal record for Hauptmann, but suddenly evidence that had at one point seemed disjointed appeared to come together. For instance, in Hauptmann the police had a man who was a carpenter by trade and thus capable of

These Manhattan gas station employees are credited with giving police the lead that resulted in Bruno Hauptmann's arrest.

building his own ladder. Hauptmann even lived in the neighborhood of the lumberyard from which it appeared the ladder's wood had come. Moreover, Hauptmann was German, which fit the profile police had of the ransom note writer. And, most damning of all, Hauptmann apparently was spending the Lindbergh ransom money, and the description of the spender's physical appearance dovetailed perfectly with Condon's description of the "John" to whom the ransom money had been delivered. Police decided it would be best to arrest Hauptmann on the street rather than at his home because it might take awhile to obtain warrants for his home. Besides, they thought that, if they arrested Hauptmann away from home, he might have his wallet with a ransom bill in it, which would be even stronger evidence that he was connected with the kidnapping.

Hauptmann Arrested

That evening, police fanned out through the Bronx neighborhood where Hauptmann lived. Hauptmann's home at 1279 East 222nd Street was just a mile from where Condon had met with the kidnapper the first time. His home also was less than four miles from where Condon had given the kidnapper the ransom money.

The next morning, Hauptmann emerged from his home, got in his car, and drove away. Officers in three cars tailed him, finally pulling him over. Hauptmann was removed from the car and handcuffed. One officer retrieved Hauptmann's wallet, in which he found a twenty-dollar gold note that had been folded into eight sections. That bill checked out as part of the Lindbergh ransom money. The officers were certain that Bruno Richard Hauptmann was their man.

Officers next obtained a warrant and searched Hauptmann's home, where they found some gold coins, which were not part of the ransom payment. They then searched Hauptmann's garage,

---

Following his arrest, Bruno Hauptmann (left) is fingerprinted by police. Officers next searched Hauptmann's home and found incriminating evidence.

where they eventually found secreted gold certificates, all of which checked out as Lindbergh ransom bills. In an attempt to try to find more ransom money, officers also examined the attic over Hauptmann's apartment and found a missing plank. The missing board appeared to match rail sixteen. Finally, officers examining closets in the apartment found writing on some trim. There, in Hauptmann's handwriting, were Condon's address and phone number. Police were more than ever convinced of Hauptmann's guilt. However, Hauptmann refused to confess.

Hauptmann's "Fisch Story"

Officers were sure they would be able to wear him down, but Hauptmann continued to claim that the cash had been left in his care by a friend and business partner, Isidor Fisch, who had subsequently died. The cash had been secured in a shoe box, which Hauptmann placed in a closet. Hauptmann said he never opened the box until the closet leaked. While moving items from the wet closet, he discovered the money, subsequently stashing it in his garage. The police, however, found the story too convenient and hence unconvincing.

On Tuesday, October 8, 1934, Bruno Richard Hauptmann was indicted by a New Jersey grand jury on a charge of murdering twenty-month-old Charles Augustus Lindbergh Jr. The indictment charged that

> Bruno Richard Hauptmann on the first day of March, in the year of our Lord one thousand nine hundred and thirty-two, with force and arms, at the Township of East Amwell, in the County of Hunterdon aforesaid, and within the jurisdiction of this court, did wilfully, feloniously and of his malice aforethought, kill and murder Charles A. Lindbergh, Jr., contrary to the form of the statute in such case made and provided and against the peace of the State, the government and the dignity of the same.[26]

The police and prosecutors had convinced a grand jury that Hauptmann should stand trial for murder. Now they had to convince a jury of his guilt.

Chapter 3

An Avalanche of Evidence

DESPITE HAUPTMANN'S STEADFAST denials of guilt, prosecutors believed they had an extraordinarily strong case. Although nobody had been able to place Hauptmann in the Lindberghs' house, the authorities had amassed a mountain of circumstantial evidence—more than enough, prosecutors believed, to prove Hauptmann guilty of Charlie's kidnapping and murder.

Hauptmann's trial was set for January 2, 1935, and by New Year's Day the town of Flemington, New Jersey, the Hunterdon County seat, was besieged by sightseers, celebrities, and some seven hundred journalists who were all gathered for what the influential Baltimore journalist and social critic H.L. Mencken called the "biggest story since the Resurrection." [27] Street vendors took full advantage of the influx of people who wanted to be on hand for the trial. Some sold trinkets of questionable taste, such as replicas of the kidnap ladder; others hawked photographs of the Lindberghs.

The extraordinary media attention gave credence to the general opinion of legal scholars that it would be difficult to impanel an impartial jury. Just several weeks before the trial began, the *Law Journal* opined,

> Due to an aroused and inflamed public sentiment by reason of the prominence of the victim and the atrocity of the crime, and the unprecedented publicity which every step and phase of the investigation has been given by the

newspapers, it will be difficult to secure a jury for the trial of Hauptmann in New Jersey, the members of which shall possess the fair, impartial, and unbiased minds deemed essential to the proper administration of the criminal law.[28]

The Trial of the Century

For the press, the trial of Bruno Richard Hauptmann was one of the biggest stories of all time. The public's clamor for information was so insistent that the largest names in the journalism business all descended on Flemington, New Jersey, to cover Hauptmann's trial.

More than seven hundred news reporters and photographers flocked to cover the trial, numbers that overwhelmed the small town's accommodations. Reporters, whose ranks included some of the biggest names in journalism, converted hotel rooms, homes, and even storefronts into makeshift studios. Utility workers strung additional phone and electric wires—enough, it was estimated, to serve another small city.

Journalists were not the only ones to be drawn to Flemington for Hauptmann's trial, however. Police estimated that some sixteen thousand cars descended on the town during the first weekend of the trial. One Sunday, when Sheriff John Curtiss opened the courthouse to the public, an estimated five thousand people—double Flemington's population—swarmed into the building.

Hordes of reporters and photographers gather in Flemington, intent on satisfying the public's voracious appetite for news of the trial.

Jury Selection

The trial began as scheduled on January 2 with juror selection. Judge Thomas W. Trenchard presided. The first potential juror was dismissed because she opposed capital punishment, and Hauptmann was accused of a capital crime. A young farmer who claimed he had never heard of the Lindbergh kidnapping or of Hauptmann was also dismissed. Several other potential jurors were dismissed by the defense on the grounds that they had been influenced by the radio and newspaper commentators who had already indicated that they considered Hauptmann guilty.

By the end of the day, however, ten jurors had been selected: Charles A. Walton, a machinist and former semiprofessional baseball player; Rosie Pill, a widow; Verna Snyder, a housewife; Charles F. Snyder, a farmer; Ethel Stockton, a legal stenographer; Elmer Smith, an insurance salesman; Robert Cravatt, a twenty-eight-year-old high school teacher; Philip Hockenbury, a truck driver; George Voorhees, a farmer; and Mary F. Brelsford, a housewife.

After the court's work was completed for the day, the selected jurors were ordered sequestered and sent to quarters on the third floor of the Union Hotel. They were instructed not to discuss the case with outsiders, read about the case in the papers, or listen to news about it on the radio. Once jurors were escorted away, Hauptmann was taken back to his cell. Hauptmann's lead attorney, Edward J. Reilly, pronounced himself satisfied with the jurors so far. "I have held the belief all along that the defendant would have as fair a trial in Flemington as he could get anywhere in the world,"[29] Reilly said.

"This Is My First Criminal Case"

Two more jurors needed to be selected the next day. With little fanfare, Howard V. Biggs, an unemployed accountant, and Liscom C. Case, a retired carpenter, were selected as the final jurors.

The court was now ready to hear the prosecution's case. New Jersey attorney general David T. Wilentz was the chief prosecutor in the case. Although the Hunterdon County district attorney would ordinarily have tried the matter, the county was unable to

The first day of jury selection for the Hauptmann trial yielded ten jurors, pictured here with officials as they leave their hotel for the courtroom.

foot the bill for what promised to be an expensive trial. The state had to take the case, and Wilentz decided to prosecute the case personally. Wilentz approached the jurors as he began his opening statement. "This is my first criminal case. I came here because it was my duty as attorney general, not because I wanted to prosecute a man for murder,"[30] he told jurors.

Wilentz then outlined the prosecution's view of the case. He began by stating that he would prove that Hauptmann alone had kidnapped Charlie, written the ransom notes, and taken ransom money from John Condon. According to Wilentz, Hauptmann had parked his car on a dirt road near the Lindbergh home and then carried his homemade ladder to the house. Wilentz said Hauptmann climbed the ladder, entered Charlie's room, snatched him from his crib, placed him in a burlap sack, and left the way he had come. Wilentz then concluded that as Hauptmann climbed down, the ladder broke, and that in the ensuing fall Charlie was fatally injured. He said, "In the commission of

TRIAL SOUVENIRS

Residents of tiny Flemington did the best they could to cope with the influx of media and visitors on hand for Hauptmann's trial. Some rented spare rooms to visitors, and the local country club was rented to a New York newspaper to house its legions of personnel sent to cover the trial.

While some residents became innkeepers for the duration of the trial, others looked to benefit financially by selling souvenirs of the proceedings. Entrepreneurs peddled everything from replicas of the kidnapper's ladder to photographs of the Lindberghs. As detailed by Jim Fisher in *The Lindbergh Case*, even children got into the act. Fisher said one "youngster sold locks of the 'Lindbergh baby's hair.' Sales were so brisk, the blond-headed boy was getting bald."

Vendors selling models of the infamous ladder do a brisk business.

that burglary, the child was instantaneously killed when it received that first blow [to the head]. It received a horrible fracture, the dimensions of which when you hear about it will convince you that death was instantaneous."[31]

Wilentz then argued that at that point Hauptmann had grabbed the ladder in one hand and the baby in the other. Roughly seventy feet from the house, Hauptmann found his movements too awkward with such a load and dropped the ladder before continuing on his way. After he had traveled a fair distance from the Lindbergh home, Hauptmann, knowing that the child was dead, removed Charlie's sleeping garment. He then took the corpse to a spot more distant from the home, improvised a shallow grave, and left with the baby's sleeper suit so he could continue his plan to extract ransom from the Lindberghs.

Death Penalty Sought

Wilentz concluded his opening statement outlining Hauptmann's eventual capture, precipitated by the gasoline station attendant who had written Hauptmann's license number on a ten-dollar ransom bill, and the discovery of more ransom money in Hauptmann's garage. Wilentz then told the jury that the prosecution would be seeking the death penalty in this case.

With preliminaries now out of the way, what was being billed as the trial of the century could now begin in earnest. The testimony of the first witness, however, was anything but dramatic. Wilentz first called a surveyor to the stand, who established the location of the Lindbergh home as being in Hunterdon County, New Jersey, a necessary step in demonstrating that the court had jurisdiction over the case. Drama was not long delayed, however.

Anne Lindbergh was the next witness. The bereaved mother outlined for the court her activities on March 1. Wilentz then

A heartbroken Anne Lindbergh arrives at the courthouse. Her testimony moved several jurors to tears.

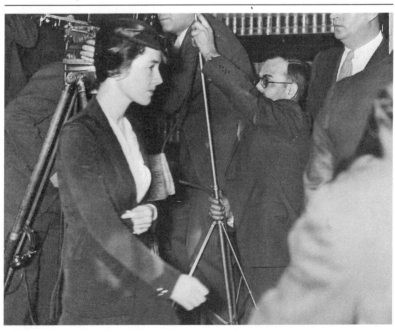

asked Anne to identify various baby garments, all of which Charlie had worn on the night of the kidnapping. As Anne made the requested identifications, several of the jurors appeared to be close to breaking down in sobs.

"Something Had Gone Wrong"

Next on the witness stand was Charles Lindbergh, who told the court that he recalled that about 9:00 P.M. on March 1, he had heard a noise that he thought was that of a slat or slats from an orange crate falling to the floor in the kitchen. An hour later, he said, Betty Gow had excitedly asked him whether he had the baby. He said he rushed to the nursery and saw the empty crib. Lindbergh said he "realized that something had gone wrong. The bedclothing in the crib was in such condition that I felt it was impossible for the baby to have gotten out himself. The bedclothing was standing stiffly enough so that the opening where the baby had been was still there—the clothing had not collapsed." [32]

Charles Lindbergh takes the stand. His testimony vividly revealed his state of mind upon viewing Charlie's empty crib.

Wilentz then got Lindbergh to identify the ransom note, asking whether it was the note he had found in the nursery. After the identification, Wilentz read the letter. Lindbergh then testified about how he attempted to help law enforcement officials familiarize themselves with the crime scene and the evening's events. At this point, Judge Trenchard decided to adjourn for the day.

The next morning, Wilentz asked Lindbergh about the events of April 2, 1932, the evening when the ransom money had been delivered. Wilentz asked Lindbergh, "On the night of April 2, 1932, when you were in the vicinity of St. Raymond's Cemetery and prior to delivering the money to Dr. Condon, you heard a voice hollering, 'Hey, Doctor'? I think. Since that time have you heard the same voice?"[33] When Lindbergh responded in the affirmative, Wilentz asked Lindbergh to identify the person whose voice he had heard. "That was Hauptmann's voice,"[34] Lindbergh testified.

Wilentz called a number of police witnesses who testified about the physical evidence they found at the Lindbergh estate on the evening of the kidnapping. Officers testified that they had seen indentations in the mud underneath the nursery window—marks that perfectly matched up with the legs of the homemade ladder they found less than one hundred feet from the house. When Corporal Joseph Wolf of the state police took the stand, he noted that there had been a footprint in the mud near the ladder indentations. He said that, comparing the print with his own shoe, he had guessed that the print was made by a person wearing size nine shoes or larger.

Hochmuth Testifies

Next called by Wilentz was eighty-seven-year-old Amandus Hochmuth, who lived near the dirt road that led to the Lindbergh home. Hochmuth testified that on the morning of March 1, 1932, he had been on his front porch when a man drove by with a ladder in his car. Hochmuth testified, "I saw a car coming around the corner, pretty good speed, and I expected it to turn over in the ditch. And as the car was about twenty-five feet away from me, the man in there looked out of the window like this

A police detective leans out of Charlie's nursery window to inspect the ladder that enabled the kidnapper to enter the Lindbergh home.

and he glared at me as if he saw a ghost."[35] Wilentz then asked whether the man who had glared at him was in the room. Hochmuth said that he was and pointed to Hauptmann. Suddenly, the lights in the courtroom went out, the result of a blown fuse. Once the lights came back on, Wilentz asked Hochmuth to make a more direct identification of the man in the car. Hochmuth tottered to Hauptmann and touched him on the knee.

Wilentz attempted several times to get the ladder introduced into evidence but was rebuffed because the prosecution had not yet conclusively linked the ladder to Hauptmann. Wilentz then put Lieutenant John Sweeney of the Newark Police on the stand to offer testimony on how the police became convinced the ladder had been used as part of the kidnap plot. Sweeney told the court that on the day after the crime, he took the homemade ladder and placed it into the indentations underneath the nursery window. The ladder fit perfectly. Moreover, Sweeney said that when placed against the house, the homemade ladder rested on two places on the wall next to the nursery window. He noticed that at these two places, the wall retained marks from having been rubbed by the ladder previously, and he noted that splinters of wood were stuck to the stone. Sweeney further testified that he used one of Lindbergh's ladders and climbed in and out of the window several times.

Wilentz followed Sweeney with Joseph Perrone, a cabdriver who said that he had been asked to deliver a letter to John Condon on March 12, 1932. When Perrone was asked whether he could identify the man who had given him the package, Perrone pointed to Hauptmann.

Jafsie Identifies Hauptmann

On Wednesday, January 9, John Condon took the stand. After establishing Condon's role in the ransom negotiations, Wilentz asked Condon whether he had given ransom money to someone at St. Raymond's Cemetery on April 2, 1932. Condon said that he had and that the man he had given the money to had identified himself as John. When asked who John is, Condon responded, "John is Bruno Richard Hauptmann."[36] The courtroom began to buzz with excitement, and reporters leapt from their seats to file the news that Condon had identified Hauptmann as the man to whom the ransom money had been paid.

On Friday, January 11, Wilentz brought Internal Revenue Service agent Frank Wilson to the witness stand. Wilson testified that he had led the effort to prepare the ransom package and noted that after the ransom had been paid, the government printed and distributed circulars that listed each of the bills that had made up the ransom package. Wilson also testified that the $14,600 in gold certificates the police had found in Hauptmann's garage were part of the ransom money, adding that no ransom bills had been found circulating since Hauptmann's arrest.

Next, Wilentz summoned Colonel H. Norman Schwarzkopf, who identified two writing samples as belonging to Hauptmann. Schwarzkopf said Hauptmann had voluntarily written the samples and that he had written what was dictated to him by a law enforcement officer. After Schwarzkopf was finished, Wilentz introduced more handwriting samples into evidence, along with the ransom notes.

Wilentz then brought a parade of handwriting experts to the stand, all of whom testified that Hauptmann was the man who had written the Lindbergh ransom notes. The final prosecution handwriting expert, Clark Sellers, concluded his testimony on January 16 by noting that Hauptmann had attempted unsuccessfully to mask his identity through handwriting. "He might as well have signed the notes with his own name," [37] Sellers testified.

Ransom Evidence Admitted

The prosecution then turned its attention to the autopsy. Doctors who had examined the corpse testified that Charlie had died of a fractured skull, causing instantaneous death.

Wilentz then sought to introduce into evidence the ten-dollar gold note Hauptmann had used at the service station, the money that eventually led to his arrest. After hearing from the gas station employee who had written Hauptmann's license plate number on the money, Judge Trenchard admitted the money as evidence. Also introduced were a pair of shoes Hauptmann had

Handwriting experts compared Bruno Hauptmann's handwriting (letters in bottom row) with samples from the ransom notes.

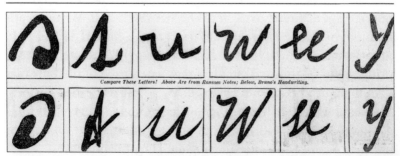

Compare These Letters! Above Are from Ransom Notes; Below, Bruno's Handwriting.

purchased for his wife, and the twenty-dollar, gold note—a part of the Lindbergh ransom package—that he had used to buy the shoes. Finally, the ransom money police found in Hauptmann's possession at the time of his arrest was also accepted into evidence.

Next, Wilentz sought to prevent the defense from claiming that the body found by William Allen was not the Lindbergh baby's. Wilentz brought in the head of a local orphanage, who testified that none of the children in her charge was missing in 1932. Hauptmann's lead attorney, Edward J. Reilly, then stunned the courtroom when he announced that the defense was not going to make a claim that the corpse was not that of the Lindbergh baby. "I will say now that there has never been any claim but this was Colonel Lindbergh's child that was found there," [38] Reilly said. The concession angered other members of the defense team. One, C. Lloyd Fisher, angrily stormed from the courtroom and said, "You are conceding Hauptmann to the electric chair!" [39] For his part, Hauptmann was heard to say, "You are killing me." [40]

Police Suspicions Aroused

Wilentz then brought FBI agent Thomas Sisk to the stand. Sisk testified about Hauptmann's arrest and how officials became suspicious that Hauptmann had hidden something in his garage. He noted that as the suspect was questioned in his apartment, Hauptmann kept sneaking looks out the window and toward the garage. Sisk then detailed the search of Hauptmann's garage.

On January 18, Wilentz brought in a former neighbor of the Hauptmanns, Ella Achenbach. After establishing that Achenbach knew the Hauptmanns, Wilentz asked whether she had seen Bruno Hauptmann shortly after the kidnapping. She said that she had, reporting that the Hauptmanns had just returned from a trip and she had exchanged pleasantries with Anna Hauptmann about their journey. Achenbach also testified that she had observed Bruno Hauptmann walking with a limp and that he had said he had sprained his ankle on the trip.

Next, Wilentz called a number of officers who had taken part in finding the ransom money hidden in Hauptmann's garage. He then called officer Henry D. Bruckman to the stand, who testified he had found Condon's address written on trim in Hauptmann's closet. The trim was admitted into evidence.

Hauptmann's Finances Analyzed

Finally, Wilentz questioned several bankers and stockbrokers who had direct knowledge of Hauptmann's finances. Although the testimony produced no bombshell revelations, it did establish that Hauptmann had amassed a large sum of money even though he was, by his own admission, unemployed.

Wilentz continued with the financial angle of the case on Monday, January 21. William Frank of the Internal Revenue Service testified that he had examined Hauptmann's finances and found that during the span of time from when the ransom was paid to Hauptmann's arrest, Hauptmann's assets had totaled $44,486.

The next day, Wilentz once again tried to get the ladder introduced into evidence. He called Lieutenant Lewis J. Born-

THE PROSECUTOR

New Jersey's attorney general David Wilentz was born in Russia but was brought by his parents to the United States when he was just a year old. Wilentz grew up in Perth Amboy, New Jersey, and there established a law firm after graduating from New York University Law School. Wilentz had become interested in politics, and after helping the successful campaign to elect A. Harry Moore as state governor, Wilentz was appointed to the post of attorney general in 1933.

Wilentz was known as a sophisticated dresser and often showed up at court wearing a white felt hat he wore with half the brim turned down. Some trial observers, including the writer Damon Runyon, found the hat an unbecoming affectation. As related by Ludovic Kennedy in *The Airman and the Carpenter: The Lindbergh Kidnapping and the Framing of Richard Hauptmann*, Runyon wrote, "His best friends and severest critics should inform the dapper gentleman from Perth Amboy that the white kady [a men's hat] is all right for [movie cowboy] Tom Mix, but not for one of Jersey's well-dressed gents."

Although the Hauptmann case represented the pinnacle of his prosecutorial career, Wilentz went on to build a successful law practice in Perth Amboy. Moreover, he remained a fixture in the state's Democratic party. Wilentz's son, Robert Wilentz, was appointed chief justice of the state's supreme court in 1979.

mann to identify the ladder, and the New Jersey State trooper said that the ladder in the courtroom that day was the same ladder that had been found seventy-five feet from the Lindbergh's house. Although the defense complained that no one had proven that the ladder had ever been in Hauptmann's possession, Judge Trenchard noted that Hochmuth had earlier testified he had seen Hauptmann with a ladder in his car. Trenchard admitted the ladder into evidence.

The Missing Floorboard

Wilentz then laid the groundwork for testimony of his wood expert by calling witnesses from several lumber companies. Then, on January 23, Wilentz brought Lieutenant Bornmann back to the stand, where he testified that while searching Hauptmann's attic, he and several officers discovered that a portion of a floorboard was missing. He told of seeing nail holes in the beams where the missing board had at one time been secured and sawdust from where the board had been cut from the floor.

Bornmann testified that on October 9, he went back to the attic with wood expert Arthur Koehler. The two matched the holes in the beams with nail holes in what they referred to as rail sixteen of the kidnapper's ladder. They found that the holes lined up perfectly and that with the board in place on the beams, they could easily slide nails through the board and into the joists.

Koehler then took the stand. He told the jury how he had traced the origins of boards in the kidnapper's ladder from the place they were milled to a local lumber store. Koehler also demonstrated that a ladder rung had been planed using a tool in Hauptmann's garage.

"Several Inches to Spare"

The following day, on January 24, Wilentz introduced into evidence a photograph of Hauptmann's car. Directing Koehler's attention to the photo, Wilentz asked whether Koehler had tried to fit the ladder into the car. Koehler acknowledged that he had, adding, "When I took the three sections and nested them together, they fit in on top of the front and rear seats, and there were several inches to spare."[41] Koehler was Wilentz's final witness. When Koehler's testimony had concluded, Wilentz said simply, "The State rests."[42]

Wilentz, however, would have much more to say, both in cross-examining Hauptmann's defense witnesses and in his summation to the jury. But for the time being, it was defense attorney Reilly who would take center stage in this drama.

Chapter 4

An Attempt to Cast Doubt

ALTHOUGH BRUNO RICHARD Hauptmann, like any criminal defendant, was presumed innocent until proven guilty, Hauptmann labored under something of a disadvantage in the court of public opinion in mounting a defense. Wilentz's opening statement had been strong and forceful. Moreover, Wilentz had produced a raft of evidence implicating Hauptmann in the crime. To counter the prosecution, Hauptmann's lawyers pursued a multifaceted strategy designed to cast doubt on the prosecution's case. They suggested that the kidnapping had been carried out by people close to the Lindberghs. This strategy was a clear attempt to offer an alternative theory of the crime. They also attacked the police investigation, which they claimed was slipshod and unprofessional and also attempted, through alibi witnesses, to show that Hauptmann was nowhere near the Lindbergh estate on the night of the kidnapping.

Hauptmann's chief lawyer was Edward J. Reilly, who came to the case after the Hearst Corporation–owned *New York Journal* made a deal with Anna Hauptmann to pay for Reilly's services in return for the exclusive rights to her story throughout the trial. Reilly was a celebrated and flamboyant defense lawyer who had defended more than two thousand clients, most in murder cases, and his success was legendary. However, though he was only fifty-two years old, Reilly was considered by many legal observers of the time to be past his prime. He had suffered an embarrassing string of losses, and some courthouse wags had begun

EDWARD J. REILLY

Bruno Richard Hauptmann's lead attorney, Edward J. Reilly, had at one time enjoyed a reputation as one of the best trial attorneys in New York City. People would go out of their way to see him argue a case.

As recalled in *The Lindbergh Case* by Jim Fisher, "young lawyers from all over town would flock to the courthouse to see him perform." Fisher continues:

> In his prime, Reilly had been a shrewd cross-examiner who quickly sensed a witness's soft spot, then zeroed in for the kill. An emotional man, he was prone to shouting, blustering, bluffing, and weeping. One moment he'd be sobbing pitifully; the next he'd be cold, sarcastic, even cruel. But Reilly's most potent weapon was his ability to appear triumphant in the face of total defeat. He had an uncanny ability to shrug off the most incriminating evidence in a way that would persuade a jury it didn't exist.

Hauptmann confers with his lead attorney, Edward Reilly.

to refer to the lawyer as "Death House" Reilly. Nevertheless, the announcement that Reilly would represent Hauptmann created a stir. Rounding out the defense team were C. Lloyd Fisher, an attorney from Flemington; Frederick A. Pope, an experienced lawyer from Somerville, New Jersey; and Egbert Rosecrans, a Blairstown, New Jersey, expert on constitutional law.

"You Are Lying!"

Bruno Richard Hauptmann and Anna Hauptmann, along with the lawyers, battled Wilentz throughout the length of the trial, a battle that included some unscripted and passionate outbursts. For example, at one point, as the prosecution elicited testimony from police about money found in Hauptmann's garage, Bruno Hauptmann shouted, "Mister, Mister, you are lying! You are telling a story!"[43]

Most of the courtroom's defense fireworks, however, came from Hauptmann's lawyers as they contested evidence and the very foundations of the prosecution's case. The defense wasted little time in trying to undermine the prosecution. For example, immediately after Wilentz concluded his case on Thursday, January 24, Egbert Rosecrans moved to have the entire case dismissed on the grounds that the prosecution had failed to prove that the baby was killed in Hunterdon County. Judge Trenchard, however, denied the motion and ordered the defense to present its case.

C. Lloyd Fisher presented the defense's opening statement. Fisher calmly told the jury that the defense would show that Hauptmann could not possibly have done what the prosecution claimed, since he was nowhere in the vicinity when the crime was committed. Fisher also promised that the defense would bring its own handwriting experts to the stand, who would testify that the notes were not written by Hauptmann. Moreover, Fisher promised that the defense would provide a reasonable explanation for Hauptmann's finances, which he claimed had been vastly overstated by the prosecution. As a matter of fact, Fisher said, Hauptmann currently was penniless. Glossing over the fact that the bulk of Hauptmann's funds had been seized by New Jersey as evidence in the case against him, Fisher said, "We will show you that the funds of this man Hauptmann are completely and totally exhausted. He is before you here in the court without one dollar that he can call his own, without a penny in the world. And his defense has been almost entirely financed through the members of his counsel."[44] In saying this, Fisher also left unsaid that the Hearst Corporation was paying Reilly's retainer.

Fisher also said the defense would expose the police work in the case as extremely poor. "We believe we will be able to show that no case in all of history was as badly handled or as badly mangled as this case,"[45] Fisher said.

Hauptmann Takes the Stand

Hauptmann was then brought to the stand. Reilly prodded Hauptmann to offer a mini-autobiography to the jury. Hauptmann discussed his hardscrabble life in Germany, how he had worked hard once he got to the United States, and how he, along with Anna Hauptmann, had scrimped to accumulate wealth.

Most significantly, Hauptmann provided an alibi for his whereabouts on March 1, 1932, the night of the kidnapping, and on April 2, 1932, the night the ransom was paid. Accounting for his whereabouts throughout the day, Hauptmann told the jury that on the evening of the kidnapping, he had driven to the bakery where his wife worked and had dinner. He then took a friend's dog for a walk as he waited for Anna's shift to end. While walking the animal, Hauptmann recalled, a man at a gas station asked about the dog. Reilly asked Hauptmann what time it was when he was queried about the dog. "Between eight and half-past eight,"[46] Hauptmann testified. Reilly repeated Haupt-

Bruno Hauptmann takes the stand. Seeking sympathy from the jury, attorney Edward Reilly asked the defendant to share details of his difficult life.

mann's words, hoping they would sink in with the jury, since the time was significant. If Hauptmann was seen at the gas station at that hour of the evening, there was no way he could have traveled to the Lindberghs' house and kidnapped Charlie. Reilly then asked Hauptmann for the second time whether he had been in Hopewell on March 1, 1932. Hauptmann replied, "I was not."[47] Hauptmann also categorically denied having received ransom money from John Condon on April 2, 1932, at St. Raymond's Cemetery. Although Hauptmann had previously said that he had not even left his apartment that evening, he now remembered that he had driven a friend to a streetcar stop at a little after 11:00 P.M. Other than that, Hauptmann said, he had been at home.

Hauptmann Denies Ransom Notes

Moreover, Hauptmann denied having anything to do with the ladder used in the kidnapping. Reilly directed Hauptmann's attention to the ladder, and after Hauptmann denied having built it, Reilly asked Hauptmann if the ladder appeared well made. Hauptmann examined the eighteen-inch gap between the ladder's rungs, then responded, "To me, it [hardly] looks like a ladder at all. I don't know how a man can step up."[48] Hauptmann went on to deny having taken wood from his attic to make a ladder rail.

Hauptmann also explained his friendship and business partnership with Isidor Fisch, which ultimately ended with Hauptmann unknowingly holding the ransom money. Hauptmann repeated that upon discovering the money, he had felt entitled to spend some of it, since Fisch had died owing him for previous loans. Hauptmann also provided lengthy testimony on his stock trading activities, with Reilly attempting to paint the picture that Hauptmann's alleged wealth was mostly a combination of shrewd stock bets and paper profits.

In other matters, Hauptmann staunchly denied having written the ransom letters. Reilly also introduced a new element to the case when he asked Hauptmann whether he had been beaten up by the police. Hauptmann responded that he had been beaten on the second evening after his arrest. Hauptmann recalled that that was the first evening the police had required him to offer writing samples.

"I Got the Treatment"

Reilly used the opening to attack the credibility of the police. Reilly asked if the police had told Hauptmann what words to write and how to spell them, and Hauptmann said they had told him how to spell some of the words he testified that the police forced him to write. Even when he dozed off, the police jabbed him and commanded that he continue. Once the writing samples were out of the way, Hauptmann said, "I got the treatment,"[49] meaning that he had been beaten.

Hauptmann also denied having any knowledge about some of the state's physical evidence. For example, Reilly showed Hauptmann Charlie's sleeper. After examining but not touching the clothing, Hauptmann denied having ever seen it.

Wilentz aggressively cross-examined Hauptmann, and rumors circulated in the press that the defendant either had confessed to the kidnapping and murder or had come very close to doing so. To counter the rumors, Hauptmann issued a statement. He said, "I was tired yesterday, yes, after six hours as a witness, but I was telling the whole truth every minute, to the best of my recollection. To make up reports about a confession is very unfair to me, because I have confessed all there is to confess."[50] Despite his calm facade, Hauptmann was bitter and glum. During a conversation with C. Lloyd Fisher, Hauptmann heard a siren from a passing fire engine. "I hope that's Dr. Condon's house,"[51] Hauptmann said.

"They're Hurting Me!"

Anna Hauptmann was next to appear on behalf of the defense, and the defense hoped that her testimony would help to establish an alibi for Hauptmann's whereabouts on the night of the kidnapping. A *New York Times* reporter wrote of Anna Hauptmann's appearance in court that day that "[s]he spoke in a thin voice with a German accent, slurring her words and using a low tone which made her voice barely audible. Although she ap-

Bruno Richard Hauptmann

Although he consistently denied involvement in the Lindbergh kidnapping, Bruno Richard Hauptmann had a history of scrapes with the law. As a young man, Hauptmann had been arrested several times by authorities in his native Germany.

In 1919, Hauptmann and an accomplice burglarized the home of the mayor of his hometown of Kamenz. In a scene eerily similar to the Lindbergh kidnapping, Hauptmann and his accomplice used a ladder to get into the house through a second-floor window. Hauptmann served four years in prison for this crime and others. A month after his release, Hauptmann was again arrested, this time for possession of stolen tools. Hauptmann managed to escape from jail before the case went to trial.

Hauptmann eventually managed to make it to the United States by stowing away in a ship. He entered the country with a stolen identification card and wearing a disguise. He later met Anna Schoeffler, whom he married in 1925. Hauptmann originally made a living as a carpenter, a trade he had learned after completing elementary school in Germany. Jobs became scarce, however, with the onset of the Great Depression. Hauptmann survived by speculating in stocks and by selling furs and other goods with a friend, Isidor Fisch. Hauptmann's stock investments grew shortly after the Lindbergh ransom had been paid, though Hauptmann always claimed that it was the shrewdness of his investments that allowed his funds to grow.

peared frightened, she was calm, and from time to time a crooked smile appeared at the corner of her mouth."[52]

The defense then put up a number of other alibi witnesses whose testimony was aimed at accounting for Hauptmann's whereabouts on the night of the kidnapping and the night the ransom money had been paid. However, they invariably had shady pasts: One, for example, had been a bootlegger, another a speakeasy proprietor, and another had been found guilty of assaulting a woman.

Although these witnesses safely placed Hauptmann in the Bronx on the evenings in question, Hauptmann himself began to believe that their testimony was doing him more harm than good. Not only were they not credible, but the witnesses made Hauptmann appear to be someone who consorted with criminals. Speaking with C. Lloyd Fisher, Hauptmann complained, "Where are they getting these witnesses from? They're hurting me!"[53]

Hauptmann added, "Tell Mr. Reilly he's got to find out if they are honest, good people before they are witnesses for me!"[54]

Alternate Theories Offered

The defense also tried to counter the handwriting analysis offered by the prosecution. On February 1, John Trendley, a handwriting expert from St. Louis, testified that after examining the ransom notes and the writings Hauptmann had provided for the police, he had concluded that Hauptmann had not written the ransom notes.

The next defense witness was Peter Sommer, a self-proclaimed fingerprint expert who said his work had imbued in him the importance of making precise observations. Sommer testified that while on a ferry running between New Jersey and New York City around midnight on March 1, 1932, he saw a man he later learned was Isidor Fisch. Once the ferry docked in Manhattan, Sommer said he saw Fisch and another man help a woman who matched the description of Violet Sharpe onto a streetcar. Sharpe, he said, was carrying a baby. Sommer went on to testify that the woman he saw seemed nervous and that when the baby's blanket slipped, he "noticed the baby was dressed in a one-piece nighty. The baby was blond, I would say about two years old."[55]

The defense had provided alibis, however questionable their credibility, for Hauptmann, rebutted handwriting evidence, and

Mystery man Isidor Fisch is pictured in an official ID photo.

had begun to offer an alternate theory of who committed the crime. Now Reilly attempted to add flesh to that alternate theory. He called a witness named Benjamin Heier, who claimed that while on a date, he had seen a man jump over the wall of St. Raymond's Cemetery on the evening of April 2, 1932. He had gotten a good look at the man's face and was startled when he saw the man's face again later in the newspapers in connection with the Lindbergh kidnapping. The man he saw that evening, Heier said, was Isidor Fisch.

Lindbergh Servants

Earlier, Reilly had used his cross-examination of Colonel Lindbergh to cast suspicion on neighbors living within the vicinity of the Lindbergh estate. His questions implied that neighbors had kidnapped the child in revenge for Lindbergh preventing them from hunting in the woods on his property. The tactic backfired, however. A bemused Lindbergh responded that no one had been prevented from hunting because he had built his house there.

Undaunted, Reilly then launched a series of questions intended to cast suspicion on the Lindberghs' servants. Reilly doggedly pressed Lindbergh on whether he had, either before or after the kidnapping, delved into the backgrounds of the family's domestic help, at one time asking, "Did you not make any effort as a father to find out the background of the people that were in the house the night your child was snatched away?"[56] Lindbergh, however, continually expressed his faith and trust in the servants and noted that the police had thoroughly checked their backgrounds.

Reilly also took aim at John Condon, and his questions left no doubt that he believed Condon must have had something to do with the kidnapping. Again, however, Lindbergh refused to take Reilly's bait. Lindbergh said that although the circumstances of Condon's involvement were somewhat odd, "we also realized that after this circumstance had originally happened the sequence of events would probably be peculiar, not according to the ordinary logic of life."[57] Despite his best efforts, Reilly had failed to get anything from Lindbergh that helped his client.

Police Work Challenged

Hauptmann's lawyer, however, kept trying to implicate those closest to the family. In his cross-examination of Betty Gow, for example, Reilly implied that Gow and some friends of hers had conspired to carry out the kidnapping. Once again, though, Reilly was unable to shift suspicion away from Hauptmann.

Reilly then set out to discredit the police investigation, and here he began to enjoy some success. When he cross-examined Corporal Joseph Wolf, for example, Reilly got Wolf to admit that he should have measured the shoe print underneath the nursery window instead of hazarding an educated guess about its size. When Lieutenant Bornmann took the stand for the first time, Reilly instantly asked him what size shoe Oliver Whateley, the Lindbergh butler, wore. When Bornmann said he had made no such inquiries, Reilly expressed surprise. "Wasn't everybody in the house that night, with the exception of Colonel Lindbergh and his wife, under suspicion?"[58] Reilly asked. Reilly had made his point. The police had failed to follow basic investigatory procedures, tainting the case from the beginning.

Reilly kept up the pressure when he cross-examined Frank Kelly, who had by this time been promoted to sergeant and who had processed the crime scene for the New Jersey Police. Once again, he castigated the witness for his failure to measure the footprint underneath the nursery window. Kelly said he thought that Detective Nuncio De Gaetano was handling that aspect of the scene and added that he had photographed the footprint. When De Gaetano took the stand, Reilly continued to hammer away at the issue of the unmeasured footprint. After getting De Gaetano to admit that he had not measured the print, he noted that the officer had estimated the print's length as twelve inches. De Gaetano said he came to the estimate after placing his fourteen and one-half inch flashlight alongside the print. De Gaetano's testimony produced the following exchange:

> Reilly: Well then, you are giving us your best guess, isn't that it?
> De Gaetano: Yes, sir, just about it.

Reilly: And you don't know whose footprint it is, do you?
De Gaetano: No sir, I don't.[59]

An Eyewitness Sticks to Story

Reilly also tried to discredit another of the prosecution witnesses. Because of Amandus Hochmuth's explosive testimony that he had seen Hauptmann headed to the Lindbergh property on the day of the kidnapping, Reilly recognized he had no choice but to attempt to destroy Hochmuth's credibility. Reilly brought up Hochmuth's age, eighty-seven, and asked the man whether he was nearsighted or farsighted. When Hochmuth responded that his eyes were fine, Reilly fired back, "I didn't ask you that, mister. You are wearing glasses. Why do you wear glasses then—to see better?"[60] Hochmuth responded that he wore glasses to help him see better at a distance. When Reilly tried to get Hochmuth to describe what the man in the car was wearing, Hochmuth was unable to say with certainty. He said he was focused instead on the man's face and eyes. Reilly realized he was getting nowhere and finally gave up questioning Hochmuth.

Reilly was more successful in attempts to keep the prosecution from introducing the ladder into evidence, noting that the ladder had been altered and had been in the possession of people the prosecution had yet to identify. When Lieutenant John Sweeney testified that he had utilized a ladder to gain access to the nursery on numerous occasions as part of a test of the prosecution's theory of the case, Reilly was ready to pounce again. After getting Sweeney to provide a detailed explanation of how he had climbed from the ladder and into the nursery, Reilly pointed out that Sweeney had needed both hands to effect the maneuver. Consequently, it was impossible to imagine that anyone could get back down the ladder using only one hand while the other clutched a sack containing an infant.

Reilly also attempted to discredit the prosecution's handwriting analysts. For example, he tried to get handwriting expert Albert S. Osborn to admit that he had made mistakes in previous cases. Osborn, however, refused to acknowledge any such errors. In the end, even Reilly's own handwriting analysts refused to testify

Officials examine the kidnapper's ladder. Hauptmann's attorney attempted to exclude this dramatic piece of evidence from the trial.

on behalf of the defense, leaving Reilly's strategy in tatters. One, Samuel C. Malone, withdrew from the case, telling reporters who asked that he had "very good reasons"[61] for his withdrawal.

"I Believe This Man Is Absolutely Innocent"

On Friday, February 8, the defense rested. All that remained to be done on Hauptmann's defense was for his lawyers to offer a summation. On February 11, as he addressed the jury, Reilly took sharp aim at the prosecution's case, claiming it was filled with inconsistencies and stretched credulity to the breaking point. For example, he said the prosecution's claim that rail sixteen of the alleged kidnapper's ladder had once been a floorboard in Hauptmann's attic was particularly ludicrous. Reilly said that Koehler would

> have you believe that this carpenter, Hauptmann, who could buy any kind of wood in a lumberyard, went out

and got two or three different kinds of wood, and then said to himself, "My goodness, I am short a piece of lumber! What am I going to do?" Whatever was he going to do? There is a lumberyard around the corner. And so he crawls up into his attic and tears up a board and takes it downstairs and saws it lengthwise and crosswise and every other wise to make the side of a ladder![62]

Moreover, though he did not directly accuse Koehler or the police of planting the attic floorboard on the makeshift ladder to frame Hauptmann, Reilly hinted as much. He said so many people had handled the ladder that it was impossible to say whether it had been materially altered.

Reilly acknowledged that some of Hauptmann's witnesses—particularly his alibi witnesses—lacked the credibility of the prosecution's witnesses. But he said a person's testimony should not be discounted simply because of a shady past. "Well, we can't go out and pick these people out of colleges,"[63] he said.

Reilly stated forthrightly that Lindbergh had been sabotaged by disloyal servants:

SEQUESTERING THE HAUPTMANN JURORS

Because of the frenzied media interest in the Lindbergh kidnapping case, the eight men and four women who made up the jury were sequestered, or isolated, from the public for the duration of the trial. They were housed across the street from the courthouse in the Union Hotel.

Judge Thomas W. Trenchard gave strict instructions to the jurors not to discuss the case with outsiders, read about the case in newspapers, or listen to reports on the case on the radio. However, there are some doubts as to how well isolated the jurors actually were.

On the Hunterdon Online website, located at www.lindberghtrial.com, the *Hunterdon County Democrat* noted that jurors

> made twice daily round trips to the courthouse through crowds of spectators calling for Hauptmann's conviction and death, and passed newsboys shouting the latest trial headlines. It is probable that they also overheard the loud radios in the taproom beneath their living quarters, and almost certain that they heard other patrons as they ate in the hotel dining room.

Colonel Lindbergh was stabbed in the back by the disloyalty of those who worked for him. A man can't come up to a strange house with a ladder and stack it against the wall and run up the ladder, push open the shutter, and walk into a room that he has never been in before. I say that ladder was a plant: that ladder was never up against the side of that house that night. Oh, it was so well planned by disloyal people, so well planned![64]

According to Reilly, the kidnapping and murder had been undertaken by Isidor Fisch, Violet Sharpe, Betty Gow, the Whateleys, and John Condon, the latter of whom Reilly said "stands behind something in this case that is unholy."[65]

Reilly said that lingering anti-German prejudice from World War I was no doubt behind the prosecution. He said, "The mob wants the German carpenter killed, as mobs for the past two thousand years have cried for the death of a person. . . . Then afterwards it was discovered that the person who was killed by the mob's vengeance wasn't guilty at all."[66]

Reilly said it was beyond belief that any one person could have committed what he conceded was a horrific crime. He said there were undoubtedly two or three culprits at large but that, in his opinion, Hauptmann had nothing to do with the crime. "I believe this man is absolutely innocent of murder,"[67] Reilly said.

Chapter 5

"We Find the Defendant . . . Guilty"

H AUPTMANN'S FATE WAS now in the hands of the twelve jurors who had been picked just a little over a month before. Hours of testimony and mounds of evidence needed to be considered and analyzed to determine whether the prosecution had conclusively proven Hauptmann's guilt.

February 13 marked the thirty-second day of Hauptmann's trial and would prove to be the last. At 9:55 A.M., Hauptmann entered the crowded courtroom with his head down and took his seat at the defense table. A reporter sitting nearby asked Hauptmann how he felt and what he thought the outcome of the proceedings would be. Hauptmann told the reporter that he felt fine but said he had no idea what verdict the jury would come to. "Your guess is as good as mine," [68] Hauptmann told the reporter.

At 10:02 A.M., Judge Trenchard entered the courtroom. In his hands were a pile of papers and a solitary yellow pencil. The jurors were already seated in the jury box beneath a large American flag. Judge Trenchard wasted no time in getting to the heart of the day's concerns, charging the jury with its duty to judge the Hauptmann case. He told the jurors,

> Ladies and gentlemen of the jury, the prisoner at the bar, Bruno Richard Hauptmann, stands charged in this indictment with the murder of Charles A. Lindbergh, Jr., in this county on the first day of March, 1932. It now becomes your duty to render a verdict upon the question

of his guilt or his innocence and upon the degree of his guilt, if guilty.[69]

Trenchard went on to remind the jurors that it was their responsibility to determine the facts of the case and to judge the credibility of the evidence and witnesses. He also reminded the jurors that in American courts, defendants are considered innocent until proven guilty and that if they had a reasonable doubt about Hauptmann's guilt, they would have to declare him not guilty. Trenchard then provided the jurors with a definition of reasonable doubt. He said that if after examining all the evidence, jurors did not feel with "moral certainty"[70] that Hauptmann was guilty, then they would have to return with a verdict of not guilty.

Evidence Reviewed

Judge Trenchard also reminded the jurors that the state's case against Hauptmann was circumstantial, since the state did not produce an eyewitness who saw Hauptmann kidnap or kill the Lindbergh baby. He added, "If the State has not satisfied you by evidence beyond a reasonable doubt that the death of the child was caused by the act of the defendant, he must be acquitted."[71]

Trenchard concluded his instructions to the jury at 11:13 A.M. He reminded jurors that they were expected to both reach a verdict and decide upon a sentence. He said if jurors found Hauptmann guilty, they had the option of sentencing him to life in prison. However, he cautioned them that if they simply

Thomas Trenchard, presiding judge at the Hauptmann trial.

announced that Hauptmann was guilty, the sentence automatically would be death.

Anne Lindbergh, still searching for solace in the aftermath of the family's tragedy, considered Trenchard's instructions to the jury to have struck the proper tone. In her diary, she wrote, "Judge Trenchard's summation is cool, dignified, wise, and infinitely removed from petty human suffering and yet relevant, just, and true to life."[72]

Reporters Reflect

Once the jurors were sent off to begin their deliberations, one of Hauptmann's lawyers, Frederick Pope, asked the judge to declare a mistrial, on the grounds that Trenchard had provided jurors with no option to find Hauptmann guilty of a lesser charge, such as manslaughter. Trenchard rejected the motion on the spot and ordered the courtroom cleared of spectators.

The lawyers in the case and news reporters, afraid to leave for fear the jury would return with a quick verdict, remained in the courtroom. As they waited, reporters began filing stories capturing the mood of those in the room. Russell B. Porter of the *New York Times* wrote,

> In the same place where laughter and noise brought a threat to clear the court, the air is hazy with tobacco smoke, men sit reading newspapers with their hats on and women perch on tables and chairs to gossip about the case. There is an incessant hum of conversation where formerly the barking of the bailiff's "Quiet, please" stopped even a whisper.[73]

Other reporters pondered their own feelings about Hauptmann's guilt or innocence. Ford Madox Ford, a special correspondent for the *New York Times*, wrote that if he were a member of the jury, he would vote for Hauptmann's acquittal. Among other things, Ford believed the case pitted one of the world's most fortunate and famous men against "a miserable shred of human jetsam. And there is too much class hatred in the world already and the passion for bloodshed is too keen."[74]

The courthouse vigil continued throughout the afternoon. At 3:00 P.M., jury foreman Charles Walton requested a magnifying glass. Speculation ran rampant among reporters. Perhaps the jurors wanted to compare the ransom notes with samples of Hauptmann's writing. Or maybe they wanted to look at the notes scribbled on the trim from Hauptmann's closet.

Meanwhile, the Lindberghs gathered at the Morrow estate and waited like everyone else to hear Hauptmann's fate. Hauptmann himself was visibly worried, pacing nervously in his cell as a noisy crowd gathered outside the jail yelling, "Kill Hauptmann! Kill Hauptmann! Kill Hauptmann!"[75] At 9:00 P.M., jurors requested cigarettes.

Hauptmann Found Guilty

Finally, at 10:28 P.M., court officers announced that the jury had reached a verdict, and participants in the trial converged on the courthouse. At 10:30, the jury filed into the jury box, and one minute later, Hauptmann was led into the courtroom. At 10:40, Judge Trenchard entered the courtroom. After instructing the jury and Hauptmann to stand, Trenchard asked the jury if it had agreed upon a verdict. Charles Walton, the foreman, spoke for the jury, answering, "Guilty. We find the defendant, Bruno Richard Hauptmann, guilty of murder in the first degree."[76] After being satisfied that the jury was truly unanimous in its verdict and that the jury had not decided to give Hauptmann life in prison instead of executing him, Trenchard announced Hauptmann's death sentence. "The sentence of the court is that you, the said Bruno Richard Hauptmann, suffer death at the time and place and in the manner provided by law,"[77] Trenchard said. As Hauptmann was led from the courtroom at 10:50 P.M., C. Lloyd Fisher hurried to his side to remind Hauptmann that the court's decision that day would be challenged. Fisher said, "Remember, it's only the beginning."[78]

The Lindberghs heard the news over the radio. Harold Nicolson, a family friend who was writing a biography of Dwight Morrow, was with the Lindberghs at the time. He recalled in a letter that Colonel Lindbergh said of the verdict: "There is no doubt at all that Hauptmann did the thing. My one dread all these years has been that they would get hold of someone as a victim about whom I wasn't sure. I am sure about this—quite sure." [79] For her part, Anne Lindbergh wrote in her diary that she and her husband must try to get on with their lives. "The trial is over. We must start our life again, try to build it securely," [80] she wrote.

As the Lindberghs struggled to rebuild their lives, Hauptmann's lawyers were busy trying to save his. Reilly approached

Under sentence of death, a composed Bruno Hauptmann poses in his Hunterdon County jail cell.

Hauptmann and suggested that he might be able to avoid electrocution if he confessed. Hauptmann replied that he had nothing to confess. Reilly then went before reporters gathered outside the jail and told them that he continued to believe in Hauptmann's innocence. However, he said, he was forced to appeal to the American public for funds to mount an appeal.

Reilly Fired

Hauptmann was transferred to the New Jersey State Prison in Trenton on Saturday, February 16. He was assigned prisoner number 17,400, processed, and led to the death house before being placed in cell number nine. In the meantime, Fisher, Pope, and Rosecrans worked on an appeal, and Fisher convinced Judge Trenchard to require the state to pay for the cost of typing the trial transcript. Reilly, however, would have no part in the appeal process. Anna Hauptmann eventually fired Reilly when the lawyer presented her with a bill for $25,000.

On May 10, Fisher, Pope, and Rosecrans filed Hauptmann's appeal with the New Jersey Court of Errors and Appeals, the state's top court. The lawyers pointed to 193 points of law that they said justified a reversal of Hauptmann's conviction. Among other things, the appeal said Wilentz had improperly appealed to the jurors' emotions when he referred to Hauptmann as "Public Enemy Number One of this World."[81] Moreover, Hauptmann's lawyers argued that pretrial publicity and the carnival-like atmosphere in Flemington prevented Hauptmann from receiving a fair trial.

Following oral arguments before the appeals court on June 20, in which Rosecrans attacked the prosecution's case and Judge Trenchard's handling of the trial, Rosecrans summed up, "The question is not whether Hauptmann is guilty or innocent, it is whether he had received a fair trial."[82] Wilentz made a one-hour rebuttal, and at 4:00 P.M. the appeals court judges adjourned.

Conviction Upheld

On October 9, the fourteen judges on the appeals court unanimously upheld Hauptmann's conviction, saying that they were satisfied that Hauptmann had received a fair trial and that he

LINDBERGH KIDNAPPING LAW

The kidnapping and murder of Charles A. Lindbergh Jr. had an impact on Americans in ways both large and small. Many grieved, and others worried about the safety of their own children. Still others were spurred to action.

In the wake of the kidnapping, pressure built for Congress to make kidnapping a federal crime. As recounted in *Kidnap: The Story of the Lindbergh Case*, by George Waller, the *New York Times* noted, "Immediate pressure for early passage of the measure making kidnaping a Federal offense is held certain as the result of the kidnaping of Colonel Lindbergh's son." However, others were not so sure. According to Waller's *Kidnap*, the famous scientist Albert Einstein downplayed the effectiveness of a new federal law. According to Einstein, "Kidnaping is a sign of lack of sanity in social development and not a lack of laws."

Einstein's opinion notwithstanding, on June 22, 1932, Congress voted to make kidnapping a federal crime. Under the measure, which was known as the Lindbergh Law, any kidnapping in which the victim was not returned within a week was presumed to have involved taking the victim across state lines. Consequently, the Federal Bureau of Investigation would have jurisdiction in the matter, and anyone convicted under the statute faced a maximum penalty of life in prison.

Not completely satisfied with their work, lawmakers in 1933 amended the law. Under the revised measure, the death penalty could be imposed if the kidnapping victim was harmed. In addition, the revisions allowed the FBI to get involved in the case within twenty-four hours of the crime.

was, in fact, guilty. Now, Hauptmann's fate lay in the hands of the United States Supreme Court.

As Fisher prepared an appeal to the Supreme Court, Hauptmann requested an interview with New Jersey governor Harold G. Hoffman. On October 16, Hoffman visited Hauptmann at the death house. After thanking Hoffman for visiting him, Hauptmann complained, "Governor, why does your state do this to me? Why do they want my life for something somebody else has done?"[83] Hauptmann repeated his claim that he had been railroaded by police and prosecutors and detailed how he had been beaten by police after being arrested. Hoffman, who had come in hopes of getting a confession from Hauptmann, left.

On December 9, the U.S. Supreme Court announced it would not review Hauptmann's case. So far as the high court was concerned, the verdict would stand. Hauptmann now appealed to the New Jersey Court of Pardons, which had the power to reduce Hauptmann's sentence to life in prison. The pardon panel heard the appeal on January 11, 1936. After Wilentz provided an overview of the trial, Fisher provided several witnesses to speak on Hauptmann's behalf. Fisher then pleaded with the pardons court to spare Hauptmann's life. After a brief recess, the court was called back into session. Only one member of the court, Governor Hoffman, who had been impressed by Hauptmann's assertions of innocence when they met, voted against the execution.

Hoffman Seeks Confession

In a last-ditch effort to save Hauptmann's life, a new appeal was filed, this time with the federal appeals court in Trenton, on the grounds that Hauptmann had not received a fair trial. Because the U.S. Supreme Court had already refused to review the constitutionality of Hauptmann's conviction, it was unlikely that a lower federal court would agree to hear the matter. Indeed, on January 14, Judge J. Warren Davis announced that the court would not review the matter. In so doing, Davis noted that Hauptmann's lawyers had done their jobs. "If the prisoner goes to the electric chair he cannot blame his counsel, because they have done all that capable, earnest, industrious counsel can do,"[84] he said.

Hoffman decided to give Hauptmann one last chance at leniency in exchange for a confession. However, he did not want to risk a political firestorm by going against the wishes of the state's attorney general. Hoffmann asked Wilentz whether he would object to allowing Hauptmann to serve a life sentence instead of facing execution, provided he confessed. When Wilentz agreed, Hoffman approached Anna Hauptmann on January 16. He told Anna that unless her husband confessed, he would be executed the following day. When she protested her husband's innocence, Hoffman replied, "I know that's what you believe, Mrs. Hauptmann, but you'll have to face reality. Richard's life is at stake. If we don't do something bold and dramatic Richard

Concerned about the fairness of Hauptmann's trial, New Jersey governor Harold Hoffman signs a thirty-day reprieve for the condemned man.

will be electrocuted—tomorrow night. Let him know that you want him to confess because if he doesn't, he'll be killed."[85] Anna Hauptmann refused, continuing to say that her husband was innocent. However, she did agree to talk with Hauptmann to see if he would be willing to meet with the governor and attorney general. After speaking with his wife, Hauptmann agreed to the meeting, but stressed that he had nothing new to say.

At 4:00 P.M. that day, Hoffman held a press conference and announced he was giving Hauptmann a thirty-day reprieve. Hoffman said that he was still wrestling with the case and was not clearly convinced that Hauptmann alone was responsible for the crime. He wanted more time to study the issue before a sentence that could never be undone—death—was carried out. Hoffman said, "A human life is at stake. As governor of New Jersey I have a duty to perform. It is my heart, my conscience, my job—and this is my decision."[86]

Hoffman Denounced

Hoffman's action attracted immediate denunciation. On its front pages, the *Trenton Times* carried an editorial calling for Hoffman's impeachment, saying the governor had "dishonored himself, disgraced the state, and converted New Jersey into [an] international laughing stock."[87] Startled by the reaction, Hoffman issued a statement on January 17. In it he said that he had "never expressed an opinion upon the guilt or innocence of Hauptmann." Nevertheless, Hoffman said he was troubled by some of the evidence in the case and stated his belief that Hauptmann may not have enjoyed a fair trial because of adverse pretrial publicity. Moreover, he said, "I do doubt that this crime could have been committed by any one man, and I am worried about the eagerness of some of our law enforcement agencies to bring about the death of this one man so that the books can be closed in the thought that another great crime mystery had been successfully solved."[88]

"I WILL GO GLADLY"

Three days before being executed, on March 31, 1936, Bruno Richard Hauptmann wrote a letter to New Jersey governor Harold G. Hoffmann. Hauptmann said that whatever happened to him, he felt compelled to ask the state to continue investigating the Lindbergh kidnapping and murder. Protesting his innocence to the end, Hauptmann said his conviction and impending execution had not truly solved the crime.

As related in Jim Fisher's *The Lindbergh Case,* Hauptmann wrote:

> Your Excellence: My writing is not for fear of losing my life, this is in the hands of God, it is His will. I will go gladly, it means the end of my tremendous suffering. Only in thinking of my wife and my little boy, that is breaking my heart. I know until this terrible crime is solvet, they will have to suffer unter the weight of my unfair conviction.

> I beg you, [and the] Attorney General, believe at least a dying man. Please investigate, because the case is not solvet, it only adds another death to the Lindbergh case.

> I thank your Excellence, from the bottom of my heart, and may God bless you,

> Respectfully, Bruno Richard Hauptmann

By the end of March, however, Hoffman had lost hope of getting Hauptmann to confess and to name accomplices. Hauptmann was scheduled to be electrocuted on March 31. On March 30, the state court of pardons, in keeping with state law, met one last time to reconsider Hauptmann's request for leniency. C. Lloyd Fisher asked the panel to consider the case "with cool and calm deliberation—deliberation that is not incited by the cry of the mob, nor by an overwhelming desire on the part of police officials to clear from their records a matter which has been baffling and embarrassing." [89] At 4:00 P.M., the panel adjourned to consider the matter and at 5:00 P.M. returned to announce its decision. Hauptmann's request for clemency was denied; this time, Hoffman voted to deny Hauptmann's plea.

Hauptmann still received a last-minute reprieve, however, when a man named Paul H. Wendel said he was responsible for the Lindbergh kidnapping. Hauptmann's execution was put off until Friday, April 3.

"A World Which Has Not Understood Me"

On April 2, the grand jury investigating the Wendel matter concluded that Wendel had nothing to do with the Lindbergh kidnapping. Nothing stood in the way of Hauptmann's execution. On April 3, 1936, Fisher visited with Hauptmann one last time, and Hauptmann handed him a statement, written in German, to be distributed to the press after the execution. In it, Hauptmann expressed relief that his "life in a world which has not understood me has ended" [90] and expressed his hope that others might examine his case and conclude that capital punishment should be abolished. Hauptmann also, for the last time, protested his innocence.

Hauptmann was led from his cell to the execution chamber and was strapped into the electric chair. At 8:44 P.M., the switch was thrown. He was pronounced dead at 8:47 P.M. Afterward, C. Lloyd Fisher told reporters, "This is the greatest tragedy in the history of New Jersey. Time will never wash it away." [91]

Despite Hauptmann's conviction and subsequent execution, debate has continued as to whether Hauptmann was indeed guilty, or if he was guilty, whether he was the only person involved in the kidnapping and murder of the Lindberghs' baby. Pointing to Hauptmann's refusal to offer a confession in exchange for his life, some observers claim that only a truly innocent man would choose death.

Fisch Involved?

Proponents of such theories suggest, among other things, that Hauptmann's claims about Isidor Fisch's involvement should have been given more weight. Although the defense never came up with evidence that Fisch was involved in the crime, many believe Fisch somehow had something to do with the kidnapping and murder. Hauptmann himself, however, may have undermined such claims. He testified that he, not Fisch, had made shrewd stock investments and that he had often executed stock transactions on Fisch's behalf. To many who are convinced of Hauptmann's guilt, the resulting portrait of Fisch is that of a man incapable of plotting such a crime.

Pro-Hauptmann theorists also point to shortcomings in the police investigation to suggest that Hauptmann may have been framed. Police, for example, failed to take plaster casts of the footprints found underneath the nursery window. Had they done so, they could have compared the prints with Hauptmann's shoes or, at the very least, compared the size of the print with Hauptmann's shoe size. However, police even failed to take an accurate measurement of the prints. More diligent police work could at least have strengthened the circumstantial evidence against Hauptmann or eliminated him as a suspect. Likewise, the missing floorboard in Hauptmann's attic was discovered relatively late in the investigation. Moreover, the discovery was made by an officer who was temporarily living in Hauptmann's apartment. Some speculate that the officer cut the board himself, disassembled the kidnapper's ladder, and affixed the floorboard onto the ladder. However, others note that the federal wood expert, Koehler, had already catalogued the ladder's component parts and noted the peculiarities of that board.

As fantastic and dubious as some of the pro-Hauptmann arguments may sound, or how easily they crumble when con-

ANNA HAUPTMANN

Although the conviction and execution of Bruno Richard Hauptmann for the kidnapping and murder of Charles A. Lindbergh Jr. ostensibly closed the book on the case, Hauptmann's widow kept the matter alive by protesting her husband's innocence until her death in 1994.

Anna Hauptmann devoted her life to the attempt to clear her husband's name. In 1991, at the age of ninety-two, she returned to Hunterdon County for the first time since the trial. As related by journalist Phyllis Plitch in "Widow Comes Back to Flemington to Say Again That Bruno Was Innocent," in the *Hunterdon County Democrat*, found at Hunterdon Online, www.lindberghtrial.com, Anna said, "I'm here again today fighting for my husband. He was innocent, as innocent as you and me. My husband was innocent, and God knows it. Is there really a God in heaven?"

That same year, Anna unsuccessfully urged then New Jersey governor Jim Florio to reexamine the case and clear her husband's name.

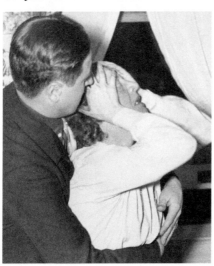

Anna honored her husband's memory in ways both large and small. As recalled in "Anna Hauptmann's Crusade," in the *Hunterdon County Democrat* at Hunterdon Online, www.lindberghtrial.com, she refused to say the words "liberty and justice for all" when reciting the Pledge of Allegiance to the Flag.

After learning of her husband's death, Anna Hauptmann is comforted by a reporter.

fronted with the case's facts, historian and author Jim Fisher offers a theory on why such protests persist. In *The Ghosts of Hopewell: Setting the Record Straight in the Lindbergh Case,* Fisher said, "Americans tend to be more interested in injustice than justice, [so] it's hard for writers to resist turning cold-blooded killers into victims of heavy-handed prosecutors and cops." [92]

After analyzing evidence in the case, Fisher offers a conclusion that most serious scholars of the Lindbergh case share, asserting that

> the evidence not in dispute . . . is enough to prove, beyond a reasonable doubt, that Bruno Richard Hauptmann kidnapped and killed the Lindbergh baby. No one saw him snatch the baby from the crib, and no one, save the killer, witnessed the child's death. Hauptmann did not confess. Nevertheless, it is reasonable to infer that he did it for the money and as hard as it is to accept, he did it alone.[93]

Notes

Introduction: "On the Front Page of a Newspaper"

1. Quoted in Susan Hertog, *Anne Morrow Lindbergh: Her Life*. New York: Nan A. Talese, 1999, p. 77.
2. Quoted in Ludovic Kennedy, *The Airman and the Carpenter: The Lindbergh Kidnapping and the Framing of Richard Hauptmann*. New York: Viking, 1985, p. 41.
3. Quoted in Kennedy, *Airman and Carpenter*, pp. 42–43.

Chapter 1: The Crime of the Century

4. Quoted in Kennedy, *Airman and Carpenter*, p. 53.
5. Quoted in Jim Fisher, *The Lindbergh Case*. New Brunswick, NJ: Rutgers University Press, 1987, p. 12.
6. Quoted in Kennedy, *Airman and Carpenter*, p. 53.
7. Quoted in Fisher, *Lindbergh Case*, p. 18.
8. Quoted in Jim Fisher, *The Ghosts of Hopewell: Setting the Record Straight in the Lindbergh Case*. Carbondale, IL: Southern Illinois University Press, 1999, p. 7.
9. Quoted in Fisher, *Lindbergh Case*, p. 32.
10. Quoted in Fisher, *Lindbergh Case*, p. 32.
11. Quoted in George Waller, *Kidnap: The Story of the Lindbergh Case*. New York: Dial Press, 1961, p. 31.
12. Quoted in Fisher, *Lindbergh Case*, p. 42.
13. Quoted in Fisher, *Lindbergh Case*, p. 42.
14. Quoted in Fisher, *Lindbergh Case*, p. 49.
15. Quoted in Fisher, *Lindbergh Case*, p. 63.
16. Quoted in Fisher, *Ghosts of Hopewell*, p. 14.
17. Quoted in Fisher, *Ghosts of Hopewell*, p. 14.
18. Quoted in Fisher, *Lindbergh Case*, p. 67.
19. Quoted in Fisher, *Ghosts of Hopewell*, p. 19.
20. Quoted in Fisher, *Lindbergh Case*, p. 83.

Chapter 2: A Trail of Dead Ends and False Leads

21. *New York Times*, "Lindbergh Baby Kidnapped from Home of Parents on Farm Near Princeton; Taken from His Crib; Wide Search On," March 2, 1932. www.nytimes.com.
22. Quoted in Fisher, *Lindbergh Case*, p. 23.
23. Quoted in Fisher, *Lindbergh Case*, p. 49.

24. Quoted in Kennedy, *Airman and Carpenter*, p. 145.
25. Quoted in Kennedy, *Airman and Carpenter*, p. 145.
26. Quoted in Waller, *Kidnap*, p. 274.

Chapter 3: An Avalanche of Evidence

27. Quoted in Hunterdon Online, "The Trial of the Century," *Hunterdon County Democrat*, 2001. www.lindberghtrial.com.
28. Quoted in Waller, *Kidnap*, p. 281.
29. Quoted in Hunterdon Online, "The Jury," *Hunterdon County Democrat*, 2001. www.lindberghtrial.com.
30. Quoted in Fisher, *Lindbergh Case*, p. 276.
31. Quoted in Fisher, *Lindbergh Case*, p. 276.
32. Quoted in Waller, *Kidnap*, p. 289.
33. Quoted in Fisher, *Lindbergh Case*, p. 281.
34. Quoted in Fisher, *Lindbergh Case*, p. 281.
35. Quoted in Waller, *Kidnap*, p. 318.
36. Quoted in Fisher, *Lindbergh Case*, p. 293.
37. Quoted in Fisher, *Lindbergh Case*, p. 305.
38. Quoted in Fisher, *Lindbergh Case*, p. 315.
39. Quoted in Waller, *Kidnap*, p. 351.
40. Quoted in Kennedy, *Airman and Carpenter*, p. 282.
41. Quoted in Fisher, *Lindbergh Case*, p. 322.
42. Quoted in Fisher, *Lindbergh Case*, p. 323.

Chapter 4: An Attempt to Cast Doubt

43. Quoted in Kennedy, *Airman and Carpenter*, p. 282.
44. Quoted in Kennedy, *Airman and Carpenter*, p. 301.
45. Quoted in Fisher, *Lindbergh Case*, p. 324.
46. Quoted in Waller, *Kidnap*, p. 391.
47. Quoted in Waller, *Kidnap*, p. 391.
48. Quoted in Kennedy, *Airman and Carpenter*, p. 303.
49. Quoted in Waller, *Kidnap*, p. 399.
50. Quoted in Fisher, *Lindbergh Case*, p. 327.
51. Quoted in Fisher, *Lindbergh Case*, p. 327.
52. Quoted in Kennedy, *Airman and Carpenter*, p. 310.
53. Quoted in Waller, *Kidnap*, p. 442.
54. Quoted in Waller, *Kidnap*, p. 442.
55. Quoted in Waller, *Kidnap*, p. 441.
56. Quoted in Fisher, *Lindbergh Case*, p. 283.

57. Quoted in Fisher, *Lindbergh Case*, p. 284.
58. Quoted in Fisher, *Lindbergh Case*, p. 287.
59. Quoted in Fisher, *Lindbergh Case*, p. 289.
60. Quoted in Fisher, *Lindbergh Case*, p. 290.
61. Quoted in Fisher, *Lindbergh Case*, p. 303.
62. Quoted in Waller, *Kidnap*, p. 466.
63. Quoted in Fisher, *Lindbergh Case*, p. 364.
64. Quoted in Fisher, *Lindbergh Case*, p. 362.
65. Quoted in Waller, *Kidnap*, p. 465.
66. Quoted in Kennedy, *Airman and Carpenter*, p. 332.
67. Quoted in Kennedy, *Airman and Carpenter*, p. 332.

Chapter 5: "We Find the Defendant . . . Guilty"

68. Quoted in Fisher, *Lindbergh Case*, p. 369.
69. Quoted in Waller, *Kidnap*, p. 474.
70. Quoted in Waller, *Kidnap*, p. 475.
71. Quoted in Fisher, *Lindbergh Case*, p. 370.
72. Quoted in Hertog, *Anne Morrow Lindbergh*, p. 269.
73. Quoted in Kennedy, *Airman and Carpenter*, p. 340.
74. Quoted in Waller, *Kidnap*, p. 488.
75. Quoted in Waller, *Kidnap*, p. 490.
76. Quoted in Fisher, *Lindbergh Case*, p. 373.
77. Quoted in Kennedy, *Airman and Carpenter*, p. 344.
78. Quoted in Waller, *Kidnap*, p. 494.
79. Quoted in Hertog, *Anne Morrow Lindbergh*, p. 270.
80. Quoted in Fisher, *Lindbergh Case*, p. 375.
81. Quoted in Fisher, *Lindbergh Case*, p. 383.
82. Quoted in Fisher, *Lindbergh Case*, p. 383.
83. Quoted in Fisher, *Lindbergh Case*, p. 388.
84. Quoted in Fisher, *Lindbergh Case*, p. 394.
85. Quoted in Fisher, *Lindbergh Case*, p. 395.
86. Quoted in Fisher, *Lindbergh Case*, p. 396.
87. Quoted in Fisher, *Lindbergh Case*, p. 397.
88. Quoted in Fisher, *Lindbergh Case*, p. 397.
89. Quoted in Fisher, *Lindbergh Case*, p. 417.
90. Quoted in Fisher, *Lindbergh Case*, p. 425.
91. Quoted in Fisher, *Lindbergh Case*, p. 427.
92. Quoted in Fisher, *Ghosts of Hopewell*, p. xiv.
93. Quoted in Fisher, *Ghosts of Hopewell*, p. 161.

Timeline

March 1, 1932
Charles A. Lindbergh Jr. is taken from his crib at the Lindberghs' home sometime between 9:00 and 10:00 P.M. Upon investigating the nursery, the Lindberghs discover a ransom note. A ladder and chisel are later found on the property.

March 8, 1932
Dr. John Condon, a retired schoolteacher, offers his services as a go-between for the kidnappers and the Lindberghs.

March 9, 1932
Condon receives a reply from the kidnappers accepting his services as an intermediary.

March 12, 1932
Condon receives another letter from the kidnappers, telling him to bring the ransom money to Woodlawn Cemetery. Condon does not have the money but goes to meet the kidnappers anyway.

March 16, 1932
Kidnappers mail baby Charlie's sleeper to Condon as proof that they have the child.

April 1, 1932
Condon receives another letter from the kidnappers, setting the next day as the day the ransom money is to be delivered.

April 2, 1932
Condon and Lindbergh drive to a location specified by the kidnappers, a spot near St. Raymond's Cemetery. Condon delivers the ransom money and receives written instructions for finding the child. Lindbergh subsequently arranges for an aircraft to fly up and down the Atlantic coast in a fruitless effort to find the small boat on which Charlie is supposedly being kept.

May 12, 1932
A badly decomposed body of an infant is found in a wooded area near the Lindbergh home. The body is identified as that of Charles A. Lindbergh Jr.

June 10, 1932
Violet Sharpe, a servant for the Morrow family, commits suicide after the police interrogate her several times in an attempt to ascertain what she might have known about the kidnapping.

April 5, 1933
President Roosevelt issues an order requiring anyone holding more than one hundred dollars in gold notes to exchange them for currency not redeemable for gold. The order makes the Lindbergh ransom money, much of which was in the form of gold notes, more conspicuous, since fewer gold-backed notes are now in circulation.

September 15, 1934
A gas station attendant writes a license plate number on a ten-dollar gold note.

September 18, 1934
Police discover that the ten-dollar gold note is one of the Lindbergh ransom notes and that the license plate number is from a car owned by Bruno Richard Hauptmann.

September 19, 1934
Hauptmann is arrested, and police find that Hauptmann is carrying a twenty-dollar gold note, part of the Lindbergh ransom money, in his wallet.

September 20, 1934
Police find $14,600 in Lindbergh ransom money hidden in Hauptmann's garage.

September 24, 1934
A New York City policeman discovers John Condon's phone number and address written on wood trim in Hauptmann's closet.

September 26, 1934
Police find a gap in the flooring of the attic at Hauptmann's home and find that it matches one of the side rails of the kidnappper's ladder.

October 8, 1934
Hauptmann is indicted for murder by a grand jury in Hunterdon County, New Jersey.

October 16, 1934
Hauptmann is taken to Flemington, New Jersey, and placed in the Hunterdon County jail.

January 2, 1935
The Hauptmann murder trial begins.

January 9, 1935
John Condon begins his testimony, in which he identifies Hauptmann as the man to whom he gave the ransom money.

January 24, 1935
The prosecution rests its case, and Hauptmann begins his defense by testifying that he had nothing to do with the kidnapping and murder.

February 13, 1935
Hauptmann is convicted of murder and is given the death sentence.

June 20, 1935
Hauptmann's lawyers present oral arguments in appealing his conviction to the New Jersey Court of Errors and Appeals.

December 9, 1935
The U.S. Supreme Court declines to hear Hauptmann's appeal.

January 11, 1936
Hauptmann unsuccessfully pleads for leniency before the New Jersey Court of Pardons.

January 14, 1936
A federal court declines to hear Hauptmann's appeal.

January 16, 1936
The U.S. Supreme Court declines to hear Hauptmann's appeal of the federal court's decision not to intervene.

January 16, 1936
Governor Hoffman gives Hauptmann a thirty-day reprieve.

April 3, 1936
Hauptmann is executed.

For Further Reading

Robert Burleigh, *Flight: The Journey of Charles Lindbergh*. New York: Philomel Books, 1991. Recreates Lindbergh's historic 1927 trans-Atlantic flight.

David R. Collins, *Hero Pilot*. Champaign, IL: Garrard, 1978. Provides a broad overview of Lindbergh's life, including a short treatment of the kidnapping case.

The Editors of Time-Life Books with Richard B. Stolley, *Events That Shaped the Century*. Richmond, VA: Time-Life Books, 1998. Provides a broad overview of the twentieth century, including such historic events as Lindbergh's trans-Atlantic flight.

James Cross Giblin, *Charles A. Lindbergh: A Human Hero*. New York: Clarion Books, 1997. A thorough biography of Lindbergh, including a fairly detailed account of the kidnapping and trial.

Reeve Lindbergh, *Under a Wing: A Memoir*. New York: Simon & Schuster, 1998. A Lindbergh daughter movingly remembers her parents.

Blythe Randolph, *Charles Lindbergh*. New York: Franklin Watts, 1990. A thorough look at the life of the famous aviator, including the kidnapping and trial that consumed so much of his time.

Works Consulted

Books

Harold Evans, *The American Century*. New York: Alfred A. Knopf, 1998. An engaging examination of the twentieth century's signature events and personalities, including a description of Lindbergh's isolationist views during World War II.

Jim Fisher, *The Ghosts of Hopewell: Setting the Record Straight in the Lindbergh Case*. Carbondale, IL: Southern Illinois University Press, 1999. Forcefully rebuts claims that Hauptmann was either innocent of kidnapping and murdering the Lindbergh baby or had accomplices.

———, *The Lindbergh Case*. New Brunswick, NJ: Rutgers University Press, 1987. Provides a thorough, engaging, and lively account of the Lindbergh kidnapping case, from the night of the crime to Hauptmann's execution.

Susan Hertog, *Anne Morrow Lindbergh: Her Life*. New York: Nan A. Talese, 1999. A revealing portrait of Anne Lindbergh and her feelings and actions following her son's kidnapping and murder.

Ludovic Kennedy, *The Airman and the Carpenter: The Lindbergh Kidnapping and the Framing of Richard Hauptmann*. New York: Viking, 1985. A controversial take on the evidence in the Lindbergh case, suggesting that Hauptmann was wrongly convicted.

George Waller, *Kidnap: The Story of the Lindbergh Case*. New York: Dial Press, 1961. A thorough and riveting account of the case, beginning with the kidnapping itself and ending with Hauptmann's execution.

Internet Sources

ABC News, "The Lindbergh Kidnapping: Before O.J. and Monica a 'Trial of the Century,'" 1999. http://abcnews.go.com.

BBC News, "Aviator Anne Lindbergh Dies," February 8, 2001. http://newsvote.bbc.co.uk.

F. Raymond Daniell, "Lindbergh Hopeful, Is Ready to Ransom Son; Nation's Greatest Hunt for Kidnappers Pushed; All Clues Thus Far Futile; Country Is Shocked," *New York Times*, March 3, 1932. www.nytimes.com.

Hunterdon Online, "Charles A. Lindbergh," *Hunterdon County Democrat*, 2001. www.lindberghtrial.com.

————, "Anna Hauptmann," *Hunterdon County Democrat*, 2001. www.lindberghtrial.com.

————, "Anna Hauptmann's Crusade," *Hunterdon County Democrat*, October 20, 1994. www.lindberghtrial.com.

————, "A Cast of Characters," *Hunterdon County Democrat*, 2001. www.lindberghtrial.com.

————, "Charles A. Lindbergh, Jr.," *Hunterdon County Democrat*, 2001. by www.lindberghtrial.com.

————, "The Electric Chair," *Hunterdon County Democrat*, 2001. www.lindberghtrial.com

————, "The Jury," *Hunterdon County Democrat*, 2001. www.lindberghtrial.com.

————, "The Ransom Note," *Hunterdon County Democrat*, 2001. www.lindberghtrial.com.

————, "The Trial of the Century," *Hunterdon County Democrat*, 2001 www.lindberghtrial.com.

Renee Kiriluk-Hill, "'I Am the Lindbergh Baby,' Man Says," *Hunterdon County Democrat*, March 5, 1998. www.lindberghtrial.com.

————, "Is Lindbergh Baby Still Alive?" *Hunterdon County Democrat*, July 9, 1998. www.lindberghtrial.com.

New York Times, "Father Searches Grounds for Child," March 2, 1932. www.nytimes.com.

————, "Federal Aid in Hunt Ordered by Hoover," March 3, 1932. www.nytimes.com.

————, "Four States Join Hunt," March 2, 1932. www.nytimes.com.

————, "Kidnapping Arouses Sympathy of Nation," March 3, 1932. www.nytimes.com.

————, "Lindbergh Baby Kidnaped from Home of Parents on Farm Near Princeton; Taken from His Crib; Wide Search On," March 2, 1932. www.nytimes.com.

Phyllis Plitch, "Widow Comes Back to Flemington to Say Again That Bruno Was Innocent," *Hunterdon County Democrat*, October 10, 1991. www.lindberghtrial.com.

Patrick Ranfranz, "Bruno Richard Hauptmann Biography," *Charles Lindbergh: An American Aviator 2000–2002*. www. charleslindbergh.com.

————, "Col. H. Norman Schwarzkopf Biography." *Charles Lindbergh: An American Aviator 2000–2002*. www.charleslindbergh.com.

————, "Dr. John F. Condon Biography," *Charlers Lindgergh: An American Aviator 2000–2002*. www.charles lindbergh. com.

Website

The Crime Library (www.crimelibrary.com). A comprehensive source of information on some of the world's most notorious crimes.

Index

Picture Credits

About the Author

Geoffrey A. Campbell is a freelance writer and stay-at-home dad in Fort Worth, Texas. His work commonly appears in the *Fort Worth Star-Telegram* and the *World Book Yearbook*. He lives with his wife, Linda, and the couple's boy-girl twins, Kirby and Mackenzie. Geoff is a frequent school volunteer, a certified religious education teacher, and an active youth sports coach. He loves baseball and plays hardball in both the Fort Worth Men's Senior Baseball League and the Dallas–Fort Worth National Adult Baseball Association. He has written four previous books for Lucent, including works on the Pentagon Papers case, the Persian Gulf War, Thailand, and the Cold War's impact on life in the United States.